Wolfpacks at War

Wolfpacks at War

Jak Mallmann Showell

First published 2002

ISBN 0 7110 2928 8

© Compendium Publishing, 2001

Pubished by Ian Allan Publishing

an imprint of Ian Allan Publishing Ltd, Hersham, Surrey KT12 4RG

Printed in Hong Kong.

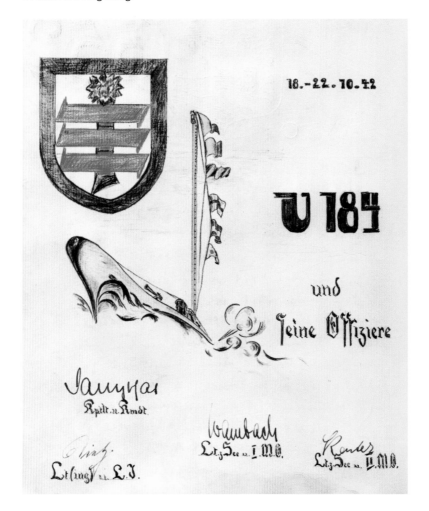

U184 under Kptlt Günther Dangschat is
a mystery boat. Its working-up period
lasted almost five months and then the
boat left Kiel on 22 October 1942 to
operate against Convoy ONS 144 off
Newfoundland. *U184* sent a radio
report on 20 November and shortly
afterwards vanished. So far, all postwar
evaluations have failed to find out why
it sank. U-boat Command posted the
boat as missing on 22 November after
it failed to respond to requests for its
position and it looks as if all the 50
men on board were killed. The boat's
motto was 'It is better to die fighting
than to rot in chains.'

Contents

Preface

Most of this book is based on unpublished documents from the U-Boot-Archiv in Cuxhaven-Altenbruch (Germany). I am most grateful to Horst Bredow (Founder and Director) for collecting the masses of information, and for guiding me through this comprehensive archive. I am also grateful to Horst Schwenk for all his assistance. The authors of the individual reports have been acknowledged throughout the book, and the original documents can be found in the archive, the majority of them being located in the appropriate boat's file.

I should also like to thank Horst Günther for helping to unravel the story of *U548*'s escape from France, Axel Katins for information supplied, and Christopher Lowe, who checked parts of the manuscript.

A good number of the photographs, especially the rare colour pictures, have come from the U-Boot-Archiv. Others have come from the author's collection. Those taken immediately after *U548*'s voyage were supplied by Horst Günther. The magnificent drawings were prepared by Richard Skinner.

It is evident that survivors from some boats made considerable efforts to reconstruct the battles they fought during the war, while others have allowed their own history to sink into obscurity. It is astonishing how many of the boats that went down with all hands actually left someone behind who escaped that final, fateful voyage, and later made a concerted effort to find out what happened to his colleagues. Sadly, many of the boats with good, detailed files in the archive did not have photographers on board or their actions took place in the dark, so that many of the written accounts cannot be supported with pictures. On the other hand, there are also the most astonishing photographic sequences without detailed captions in the U-Boot-Archiv. In this book, I have tried to marry the two together. That is, to find unpublished pictures to illustrate the stunning stories, even if the two do not show exactly the same boats. I hope readers will agree that this mishmash of an approach does help to bring the past alive.

Jak Mallmann Showell

THE 5TH U-BOAT FLOTILLA

On each spread of this book there is a panel on the right-hand page. These panels come from the 5th U-boat Flotilla visitor's book and illustrate the histories of individual U-boats.

The 5th U-Flotilla in Kiel, under Korvkpt Karl-Heinz Moehle, specialised in kitting-out and provisioning U-boats preparing for their first operational war patrol. The majority of the U-boats passed through it before going on to another unit, and so the 5th was the biggest of all flotillas. It was customary for officers of each boat to sign the visitors' book and this quickly grew into a number of volumes, which are now preserved in the U-Boot-Archiv.

The examples illustrated have been selected because they caught the author's eye—partly because some of the boats had good artists on board and produced some impressive artwork, and partly because of the stories associated with the U-boats.

The final line of each caption provides three pieces of information. WP indicates the number of times the boat left a port for war patrols. S gives the number of men who survived, and K gives the number of men who were killed, if the boat was sunk by enemy action at sea.

Left: Atmospheric shot of *U534*, today preserved at Birkenhead as a museum.

Inset: The Author at the forward hydrophone controls of *U995*.

The U-boat

THE U-BOAT ENVIRONMENT

U570, which surrendered to an aircraft in mid-Atlantic in August 1941, was floundering on an Icelandic beach when a Royal Navy inspection team appeared. They took advantage of the chance to examine at leisure the first German U-boat captured during the war. Entering the dark interior, the experts were greeted by an indescribable stench. Being submariners, they were familiar with the smell of engines, oil and other foul odours associated with the 'silent service', but this was considerably worse. Clambering down they found themselves plunged into almost knee-deep water. Mixed with it, and nicely shaken but not stirred by the recent tow through rough weather, was a generous lacing of human faeces, urine and conspicuous evidence of the crew having been seasick. Loaves of bread, a smattering of porridge oats and traces of flour were floating on top to add an unenviable stickiness to the task of wading through the evil-smelling murk.

The information in this section comes from a recently released confidential document, written for the consumption of higher officers in the Royal Navy, and therefore lacks the usual propaganda innuendo so common in reports issued to the public or for general reading within the armed forces.

At the end of the war, more inspection teams were dispatched to explore the intricacies of the German Navy. The surviving U-boats were noticeably cleaner, but even so, British submariners were not impressed, saying that discomfort inside them was generally exceedingly bad. Many of the appalling conditions came about as a result of a poor design, and they were made more unbearable by deplorable operating practices.

In his confidential report, Lt-Cdr R. A. Smith said that very few berths were provided for the crew, although the later Type XXI boats were considerably more comfortable. The worst conditions existed aboard the Type VIIC, which was the largest U-boat class ever built and the mainstay of the Battle in the Atlantic. Aboard these there were 8 bunks for 13 petty officers and 12 bunks for the remaining 25 men. The larger, ocean-going

Top: A large, long-distance boat of Type IXD2, probably *U178* or *U181*, coming into port with the attack periscope raised to act as flagpole for a mass of success pennants. The unusual patterns on the side of the hull are shadows from the reception party on the pier.

Above: *U31*, a Type VIIA, with the 88mm quick-firing deck gun in action. Cartridges were stored in a magazine beneath the radio room. They had to be passed up by a chain of men through several very small hatches and along a complicated route. Shells were stored either in waxed cardboard tubes or sealed individually inside pressure and water-resistant containers, almost as if each shell was placed inside a tin. These metal containers

were so well made that shells found in wrecks more than fifty years after the war were still in perfect condition. Although this picture is not terribly clear, the optical aiming devices can be seen on both sides of the weapon.

Above right: This is another postwar photograph showing *U995* at Laboe, near Kiel (see also page 7). Note the later version of the U-boat conning tower accommodating one 37mm anti-aircraft gun on the lower and two 20mm twins on the upper platform. The majority of large deck guns were removed from 1942 onward.

Pictures of *U995* have featured in numerous books, but this one is of special interest because it was taken by

U89

U89 was a Type VIIC from the relatively small Flender Werft in Lübeck and commissioned by Korvkpt Dietrich Lohmann on 19 November 1941. This picture—of the Pied Piper of Hamelin standing on top of the world with rats running around his feet—also featured on the conning tower as the boat's special emblem. During the night of 11–12 May 1943, *U89* was sighted by a Swordfish from aircraft carrier HMS *Biter* some six miles ahead of convoy HX237. *U89* was sunk by depth charges from the frigate *Lagan* (Lt-Cdr A. Ayre) and destroyer *Broadway* (Lt-Cdr E. H. Chevasse). *Broadway* also has the great distinction of having captured U110 under Kptlt Fritz-Julius Lemp in May 1941.

WP=5, S=0, K=48

one of the most important submarine engineers, Christoph Aschmoneit, before the boat opened as a museum. Both the raised periscopes are fitted with attack heads, which usually featured only on the aft scope. This was viewed from the inside of the conning tower, while the forward periscope, originally with a considerably larger head lens for navigation and observing the sky, terminated one deck lower down, in the central control room. The Type IX was large enough for both periscopes to be operated from the inside the conning tower. The circular radio direction finder has another aerial attached, and a bedstead-like radar aerial can be seen on the far side of the conning tower. This could be

used as an active radar set and also as a radar detector. The large bracket below the forward edge of the wind deflector held the raised schnorkel in place. Both this wind deflector and the spray deflector, half-way up the conning tower, were designed by Christoph Aschmoneit, after having got the idea from the way wind deflected around the top of the Naval Memorial. A navigation light can be seen to the right of the horseshoe-shaped lifebelt.

Above: *U415* was commissioned by Kapitänleutnant Kurt Neide and commanded by him until the end of June 1943. This was when the anti-aircraft guns were strengthened and Oblt zur See Herbert Werner, author

of the book *Iron Coffins*, took over. This shows how the 20mm anti-aircraft guns were aimed and shot. Although these guns were ineffective against large, fast-flying and armoured aircraft, their operation was relatively easy, but the gunners were not provided with protection against bullets from the aircraft.

Left: Although this shows the small conning tower of a Type II coastal boat, it does drive home the lookouts' vulnerability, especially during rough weather when water constantly washed over the top of the tower. Larger boats had more space, but the towers weren't very much higher. The lapel-less collar of the person leaning on the hatch cover indicates that he is an engineer. The pressure-resistant hatch leading into the U-boat was almost a metre below his feet, and this raised grating merely prevented men falling down the opening in the upper deck. At sea, only the conning tower hatch would have been used, but in port it was more convenient to use the lower entrances. Trees in the background and the presence of a civilian suggest that this is close to harbour.

Above right: Lookouts aboard the long-range U178 under Korvkpt Wilhelm Dommes, shortly after having left the Gironde Estuary in France to follow a small convoy through the coastal minefield. The head lens of the attack periscope is visible on the right and the raised rod aerial on the left. In later years, these aerials could be operated electrically from the inside the boat, but initially they were hand-cranked from the top of the conning tower and would not run down on their own without breaking the mechanism's sprockets. As a result, early boats were 'unfit for diving' as long as the aerial was raised. The grid by the base of the aerial was the top of a ventilation shaft leading down to the engine room. Usually there were four lookouts and a watch officer on duty on the conning tower.

Type IXC had 8 bunks for 12 petty officers and 24 bunks for some 30–34 members of the crew. Lt-Cdr Smith added that the men aboard the new Type XXI boats considered their accommodation to be on the luxurious side, and used some of the bunks as storage space. The small Type XXIII electro-boats had only two bunks for four petty officers and three bunks for the six remaining crew.

Messing facilities were also highly inadequate. The galleys were small, cramped and inconvenient to such an extent that only small quantities of food could be prepared at a time. Types VIIC and IXC had only two electric hotplates for the entire crew of between 44 and 56 men. Less than a quarter of the men could be seated for meals and the tables were located in the

main corridor through the boat, blocking the passage for anyone having to move from one part to another. The majority of men had to sit on boxes or on the floor and balance plates on their knees, making eating with knife and fork a real problem. The small number of men in each boat added to the difficulties, since everybody had a considerable workload coping with watch-keeping duties and domestic arrangements. Consequently, it was necessary to reduce maintenance work to a bare minimum and this was reflected in the poor condition of many boats.

The various operating practices aboard U-boats created atmospheric conditions which could hardly have been considered satisfactory by normal health

standards. The carbon-dioxide content, for example, usually rose to a comparatively high percentage, despite special cartridges for removing stale air. Hydrogen and oxygen detectors were not installed, although these gasses are given off in considerable quantities when batteries are charged and thus posed a significant risk of explosion. As a result, smoking was not permitted within the submarine, except in the conning tower when boats were on the surface. Air conditioning, heating and cooling systems were not provided in any of the operational boats, and it seems highly likely that the Naval Command realised this great mistake because adequate systems were later incorporated in the new Type XXI boats.

U118

U118 was commissioned with a great party atmosphere on 6 December 1941. Less than 24 hours later the news broke that there had been a massive Japanese attack on the neutral United States at Pearl Harbor on Hawaii. Four days later, Hitler declared war on the US. Immediately, the U-boat war—hitherto restricted around United States' waters—reached further west and the men of *U118* went through their training in the Baltic to the accompaniment of news from a highly successful period in the western Atlantic. Yet, these relatively easy achievements in United States' waters had evaporated by the time Korvkpt Werner Czygan led *U118* on its first operational cruise. Despite being a large minelayer, the boat was fitted out to supply smaller U-boats in mid-Atlantic, where things were already sliding down a slippery path to failure—the majority of U-boats were no longer sinking ships. Despite this, *U118* later sailed on one of the most successful minelaying operations of the war, sinking four ships to the west of Gibraltar.

WP=4, S=16, K=43

Above: This shows a small Type II coastal submarine. The main conning tower hatch can be seen open behind the periscope support, between the two men who are leaning over and peering down at the upper deck. The sailor is using the galley hatch. Much to the annoyance of the cook, this was the main way in and out of the submarine while in port. In the foreground is a red and white rescue buoy with a light on the top. This was released from a submerged boat in times of an emergency. These conspicuous objects were later accommodated inside containers with almost flush-fitting lids, to be less obstructive for men working on the upper deck. Towards the end of the war they became a superfluous luxury and some boats went to sea without them.

Above right: The central control room and nerve centre of a Type IIB, probably *U18* under Hans Pauckstadt, shortly after having been commissioned in 1936. On the man's left, and partly hidden by him, is the main steering wheel, while the other wheel operated the forward hydroplanes. The aft hydroplane controls were slightly to the right. This is not an idle shot in port but a photograph taken when the submarine was submerged—as can be seen from the hand of the large, shallow depth gauge on which the man's eyes are fixed. Fractions of metres became less critical once deeper than 25 metres, and a couple of smaller dials were provided for deeper depths. The two identical dials above the man's head, are the engine telegraphs showing both diesel engines on stop.

Towards the right is a repeater from the gyro compass with a wire running down to the deck. Near the ceiling there would also be an illuminated periscope for viewing the magnetic compass, situated inside a bulge at the base of the conning tower. Obviously, a magnetic compass would not work inside a steel submarine and so the conning tower was made from non-magnetic bronze, making it a one of the most expensive parts of a submarine.

WATCHES

Twelve men were needed to drive a Type VII U-boat, the most numerous class commissioned with over 600 built during the war. The larger, ocean-going boats of Type IX usually had 16 men on duty, but it could be driven by fewer. Since the Type VII had a complement of about four officers and 44 men, this meant that everybody had to stand at least one watch in three. To make matters worse, men of the engineering division were in even shorter supply and had to work two instead of three watches.

The watches were as follows:

00:00   First Sea Watch and Starboard Engine Room Watch go on duty.
04:00   Second Sea Watch goes on duty.
05:30   Wake Port Engine Room Watch to get ready for breakfast.
06:00   Wake crew. Port Engine Room Watch goes on duty.
06:30   Breakfast for the rest of the crew.
07:00   Clearing up, washing and maintenance duties.
08:00   Third Sea Watch.
08:45   Routine maintenance, overhaul and repair work for men not on watch.
11:30   Lunch for First Sea Watch and Starboard Engine Room Watch.
12:00   First Sea Watch and Starboard Engine Room Watch goes on duty. Lunch for the rest of the crew.
13:00   Routine maintenance, overhaul and repair work for men not on watch.
15:30   Snack for men going on duty.
16:00   Second Sea Watch goes on duty.
17:00   Evening meal for men not on duty.
18:00   Port Engine Room Watch goes on duty.
         Evening meal for Starboard Engine Room Watch.
20:00   Third Sea Watch goes on duty. Evening meal for those who have not eaten.
21:00   Silence throughout the boat for sleeping.
23:40   First Sea Watch and Starboard Engine Room Watch woken to get ready for duty at midnight.

Right and Opposite page: This remarkable and unique set of colour photographs were taken aboard *U177*, a very long-range boat of Type IXD2 under Korvkpt Robert Gysae. It operated in the South Atlantic at the same time as *U178* was close by in the Indian Ocean.

U131

'Horridoh ... the cry of the professional hunter.' The bottom line points out that an eel (torpedo) is not a Indian's arrow. Leaving Kiel on 27 November 1941, for the North Atlantic, this Type IXC boat joined a wolfpack to attack Convoy HG76, which was protected by new threat—a merchant ship converted to an escort aircraft carrier. Although *U131* succeeded in becoming the first U-boat to shoot down an aircraft (piloted by Lt G. Fletcher), it did the crew little good. Five destroyers were called in to sink the boat on its 21st day at sea.

WP=1, S=46(?), K=1

Top left and Above left: Keeping lookout was one of the most demanding and important jobs aboard a U-boat. No matter what conditions prevailed, men were expected to stand for a period of four hours at a time on the top of the conning tower scouring the horizon for enemy ships—the side that saw the enemy first was the more likely to survive.

Left: The circular device on the left is a repeater from the gyrocompass.

Today, people ask how the men endured such grim conditions. Kptlt Klaus Andersen of *U481* went some way to answering this by saying,

'It is certain that at the time I never even gave it a thought that newcomers must have suffered enormously from the appalling conditions inside the U-boat, although those claustrophobic feelings of uncertainty, anxiousness and fear were diluted the longer one was on board. People have an uncanny ability to endure harsh conditions, no matter how difficult they may be, and even consider such adverse situations as "normal". I always had great problems with the foul air. Even with ventilation fans running efficiently there were parts of the boat where the putrid air hardly stirred. I got over this problem by spending most of my time in the central control room or in the tower, where there was usually a good supply of fresh air, but the poor blokes in the bow torpedo compartment, or even worse, in the oily atmosphere of the engine room, must have suffered enormously.

'Although I served in U-boats, the question which I still cannot answer for myself is how the "Lords" actually lived in the bow torpedo room. They were squashed together worse than sardines and yet they survived without an eruption of uncontrolled aggression. In fact, I can not remember ever having to deal with disciplinary matters arising from those exceptionally cramped quarters. The senior men there, who kept those harsh quarters running smoothly, were never really appreciated nor recognised for their sterling performance.'

Right: *U124*, a Type IXB, showing the steering position inside the conning tower with voice pipe by the man's mouth. He has his hand on the button for moving the rudder to the right — there was an identical button for going in the other direction. Since it was difficult to maintain position during rough weather, operators were provided with handles to grip and thus support their bodies. One of these is visible above the man's right hand. Rudder and hydroplanes were usually electrically controlled by pressing buttons, but wheels were provided in case of a power failure. Turning these was hard work and sometimes demanded that men stood up to use both hands. If this manual mechanism broke as well, then it was also possible to operate aft hydroplanes and rudder from the rear compartment and there were duplicate forward hydroplane controls in the bow torpedo room.

Left: The navigation, or sky, periscope terminated inside the central control room—here of a small, coastal Type II. This photograph shows a war correspondent on the left, holding a microphone. The man on the right wears a leather coat with large lapels, suggesting that he is a member of seamen's division.

Right: The starboard side of the central control room with main controls for trimming or balancing the boat. One set of taps, painted green, operated the starboard tanks, while the port tanks were controlled by red-painted taps, and the trimming system was worked by grey handles. However, the colour hardly mattered, since the men who worked these had to be able to do so in total darkness. This set of interior shots of *U995* at Laboe near Kiel was taken by Christoph Aschmoneit, one of the most important U-boat designers. Although sailors maintain their own nautical language, using terms such as port and starboard instead of left and right, when it came to the crunch during an attack, they tended to identify a particular side by its colour. Incidentally, the colours can easily be remembered when one thinks of port wine being red.

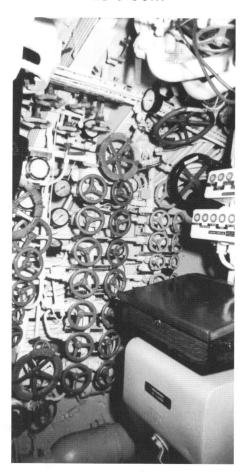

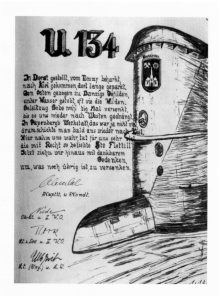

U134

Having sailed on nine war patrols, *U134* was one of the longest serving U-boats. In all that time, however, she had only sunk two or three ships—the first one was the German freighter *Steinbeck*. The first commander, Korvkpt Rudolf Schendel, had been lucky enough to have moved on when *U134* was lost with all hands. Schendel commissioned a new electro boat of Type XXI at Blohm und Voss in Hamburg on 21 September 1944. This vessel was destroyed during an air raid while lying at the shipyard. By the time the war ended Schendel was in command of a tank destroyer group on land. The second commander of *U134*, Kptlt Hans-Günther Brosin from Hannover, was aged only 26 when he died with all his crew on 24 August 1943, as a result of being depth-charged to the south of Cape Finisterre by a Wellington bomber from No179 Squadron, RAF.

WP=9, S=0, K=48

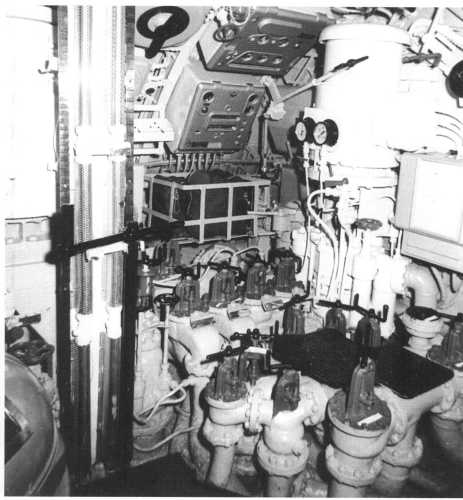

Left: The main ballast pump. Water which penetrated into the interior could be expelled with this powerful electric pump. At its base are a number of detachable covers for cleaning the inside of the pipe system.

A HYPOTHETICAL U-BOAT CREW

It is often said that Germans flourish best among a multitude of rules and regulations. The U-boats typified this, having rules to meet every possibility. The trouble was they were were fine on land, but didn't always work at sea, so a good number of boats arranged their own systems. This also had something to do with the abbreviated training received by the new men as the veterans of the prewar years died off—newcomers did not know the exact procedures laid down in the rule book and had to find their own way to cope with the various operations. There was also an unwritten rule in small boats that once someone started a job, it was usually theirs for the rest of their life or until they were given promotion. Additionally, it was often a case of boats starting their first trials with only a fraction of the crew, making it impossible to adhere to the role number system laid down by higher officialdom. Newcomers were later shunted into the less important, vacant positions. To make matters even more complicated, there were several different versions of the official roll numbers, making it only possible to give a vaguely general picture of who did what inside U-boats.

The crew list shown below is for a Type VIIC and was recently published in *Das Archiv*, the magazine of the U-Boot-Archiv.

The U-boat Crew

In addition to the crew listed below, each boat had a commander, engineering officer (the 'Chief' or LI, *Leitender Ingenieur*), first watch officer (One-W-O) and a second watch officer (Two-W-O).

During the war, when anti-aircraft armament was enlarged from a single 20mm

U172

Kptlt Carl Emmermann, one of the legendary submarine commanders, took this large ocean-going boat on five long and arduous operational tours until November 1943 when he handed it over to Oblt zur See Hermann Hoffmann. *U172* left the largest German base on the Biscay Coast, Lorient, on 22 November 1943, to be sunk a few weeks later on 13 December. *U172* attacked and sank 27 ships, making it one of the top three percent of the highest scoring U-boats. There must have been a good artist among the crew because a large version of this emblem of Neptune presiding over his realm also featured on the conning tower.

WP=6, S=46, K=13

Roll No.	Rank (Translation)	Work Station
1.	*Obersteuermann** (Navigator/Warrant QM)	Navigation table
2.	*Oberbootsmaat* (CPO)	Chief of the Boat
3.	*Bootsmaat* (Petty Officer/Boatswain)	Master at Arms
4.	*Bootsmaat* (Petty Officer/Boatswain)	Artillery section/Canteen
5.	*Funkmaat* (Radio Petty Officer)	Radio room/Paramedic
6.	*Funkmaat* (Radio Petty Officer)	Responsible for provisions
7.	*Mechanikermaat* (Mechanical PO)	Torpedo section/periscopes
8.	*Matrose* (Seaman)	Action Helmsman
9.	*Matrose* (Seaman)	Signalman with Obersteuermann
10.	*Matrose* (Seaman)	With *Oberbootsmaat*
11.	*Matrose* (Seaman)	With *Oberbootsmaat*
12.	*Matrose* (Seaman)	With *Oberbootsmaat*
13.	*Matrose* (Seaman)	With *Oberbootsmaat*
14.	*Matrose* (Seaman)	With *Oberbootsmaat*
15.	*Matrose* (Seaman)	With *Oberbootsmaat*
16.	*Matrose* (Seaman)	With *Oberbootsmaat*
17.	*Matrose* (Seaman)	Cook
18.	*Mechanikergast* (Mechanical Seaman)	Torpedo room
19.	*Mechanikergast* (Mechanical Seaman)	Torpedo room
20.	*Funkgast* (Radio Seaman)	Radio room
21.	*Funkgast* (Radio Seaman)	Radio room
22.	*Obermaschinist** (Chief Engineer/WO)	Diesel engines
23.	*Obermaschinist** (Chief Engineer/WO)	Electric motors
24.	*Maschinenmaat* (Engineering PO)	Compressors, diving, ballast, trim, and ventilation equipment. Clean and waste water systems, water still, and periscope machinery
25.	*Maschinenmaat* (Engineering PO)	Starboard diesel and auxiliary equipment with oil supply
26.	*Maschinenmaat* (Engineering PO)	Port diesel and auxiliary equipment with oil supply
27.	*Maschinenmaat* (Engineering PO)	Command systems, gyro compass, lighting, electrical equipment, consumables
28.	*Maschinenmaat* (Engineering PO)	Battery, auxiliary machinery, ventilation system
29.	*Matrose II* (Fireman)	Compressors, refrigerator, water still
30.	*Matrose II* (Fireman)	Periscope, oxygen supply, ventilation systems, fresh and waste water systems
31	*Matrose II* (Fireman)	Diving systems, ballast and trimming systems
32.	*Matrose II* (Fireman)	Starboard diesel, fuel and oil systems
33.	*Matrose II* (Fireman)	Starboard diesel, high pressure water, compressed air
34.	*Matrose II* (Fireman)	Port diesel, steam heating, high pressure water
35.	*Matrose II* (Fireman)	Port diesel, fuel and oil systems
36.	*Matrose II* (Fireman)	Command systems, gyro compass
37.	*Matrose II* (Fireman)	Command systems, gyro compass
38.	*Matrose II* (Fireman)	Batteries, auxiliary machinery
39.	*Matrose II* (Fireman)	Batteries, auxiliary machinery

* These warrant officer ranks were later filled by more senior men who were known as *Stabsoberbootsmann* or *Stabsobermaschinist*. The radio operator and the chief torpedo mechanic could also have held the rank of *Ober____* or been referred to as *Funk* or *Torpedomeister*. Some of these terms can be confusing, especially as a variety of different terms were used to describe the same positions, even during the short life of the Third Reich.
QM=Quartermaster; (C)PO=(Chief) Petty Officer; WO=Warrant Officer

Left: The diesel compartment of *U178* under Korvkpt Wilhelm Dommes showing how little space there was for the men operating the engines. Moving about the submarine, especially during choppy seas, required the skill of an acrobat—so it is unsurprising that many men were bruised and more seriously injured by being thrown against hard protrusions.

to two twin 20mm and either a quadruple 20mm or a single 37mm or double 37mm guns, then the complement rose to about 56 to cope with the additional demand. The common ranks aboard U-boats were:

Seamen (*Matrosen*)

—*Gefreiter*	Able Seaman
—*Obergefreiter*	Leading Seaman
—*Hauptgefreiter*	Leading Seaman after 4½ years' service

The dash should be replaced by the man's trade. So, the full title would have been *Maschinengefreiter, Matrosenobergefreiter* etc. 'Gast' was an old term to describe a man of the lowest rank.

These terms applied only to seamen. Trade names would have been used for other ranks, such as *Maschinist, Funkmeister, Steuermann, Mechaniker*, etc.

Petty Officers

—*maat*	Petty Officer
Ober—maat	Chief Petty Officer

The dash should be replaced with the man's trade. So the full rank would have been *Bootsmannmaat, Obermaschinenmaat, Funkmaat*, etc.

Warrant Officers

Bootmann	Boatswain
Oberbootsmann	Chief Boatswain
Stabsoberbootsmann	Senior Chief Boatswain

Commissioned Officers

Leutnant zur See	Lieutenant (Junior)
Oberleutnant zur See	Lieutenant (Senior)
Kapitänleutnant	Lieutenant Commander
Korvettenkapitän	Commander
Fregattenkapitän	Captain (Junior)
Kapitän zur See	Captain

Engineering officers belonged to the Engineering Division and had *Ingenieur* or *Ing.* after their rank.

Right: This probably shows *U108*, a Type IXB, with the earlier type of electric control panel where speed was changed by moving levers up or down. The circular hatch in the background leads through a pressure resistant bulkhead to the diesel compartment. Maschinengefreiter Hein Schmidt is working at the small desk.

U174

'The Spirit of the North in the South ...' and the tiny inscription under the heading says that many starts were frustrated by mechanical breakdowns. Launched and commissioned at Deschimag AG Weser, shortly after *U172* and *U173*, it was 30 July 1942, before *U174* left Kiel for its first war cruise to the North Atlantic. Ulrich Thilo was the commander of the Torpedo School Flotilla at the start of the war, and served in a number of other land-based positions before and after a spell in this U-boat, from 26 November 1941, until 8 March 1943. The second commander, Oblt zur See Wolfgang Grandefeld, and his crew of 52 were killed when the boat was bombed by a Ventura aircraft from VP-125 Squadron, US Navy on 27 April 1943.

WP=3, S=0, K=53

Inset: The galley of *U121*, a small Type IIB. In this boat the cook had to prepare three meals a day for 25 men, but the galley of a Type VII, with a crew of up to 56, was not very much bigger.

A typical Type VIIC—the largest submarine class ever built and the mainstay of the Battle of the Atlantic.

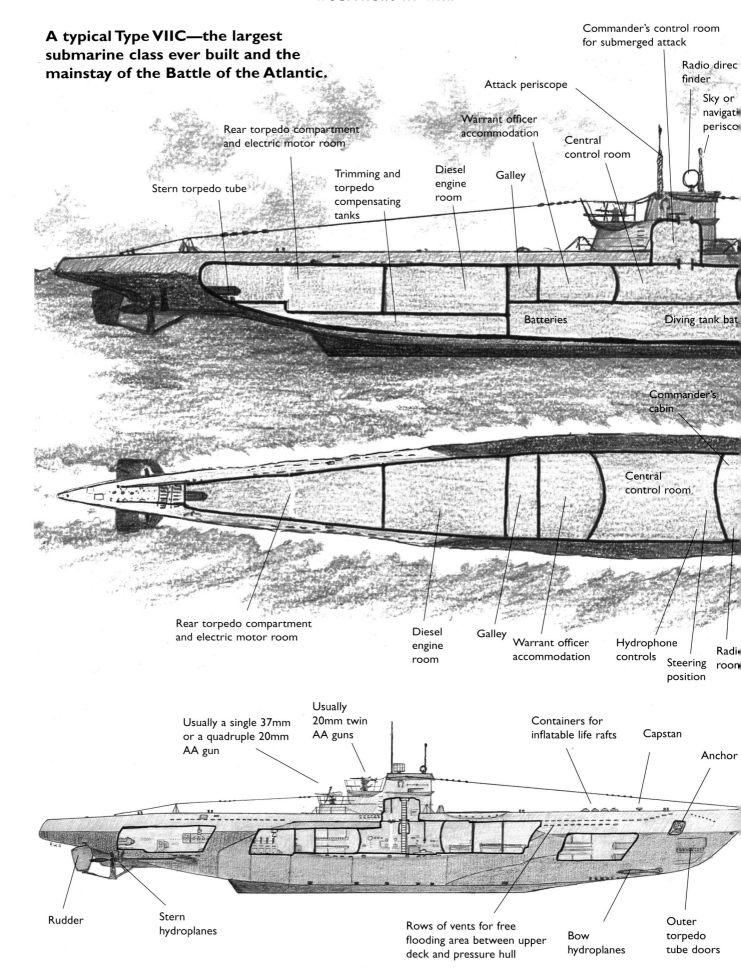

Commander's control room for submerged attack

Radio direc finder

Sky or navigati perisco

Attack periscope

Warrant officer accommodation

Central control room

Rear torpedo compartment and electric motor room

Stern torpedo tube

Trimming and torpedo compensating tanks

Diesel engine room

Galley

Batteries

Diving tank bat

Commander's cabin

Central control room

Rear torpedo compartment and electric motor room

Diesel engine room

Galley

Warrant officer accommodation

Hydrophone controls

Steering position

Radi room

Usually a single 37mm or a quadruple 20mm AA gun

Usually 20mm twin AA guns

Containers for inflatable life rafts

Capstan

Anchor

Rudder

Stern hydroplanes

Rows of vents for free flooding area between upper deck and pressure hull

Bow hydroplanes

Outer torpedo tube doors

Commander's
accommodation
and radio and
sound rooms

Bow torpedo room:
space for six spare
torpedoes and
accommodation for
the crew

Trimming and
torpedo
compensating
tanks

Officer
accommodation

Jumping wire
and radio
aerial

Head
(lavatory)

Four torpedo tubes

Officer
ommodation

Bow torpedo room

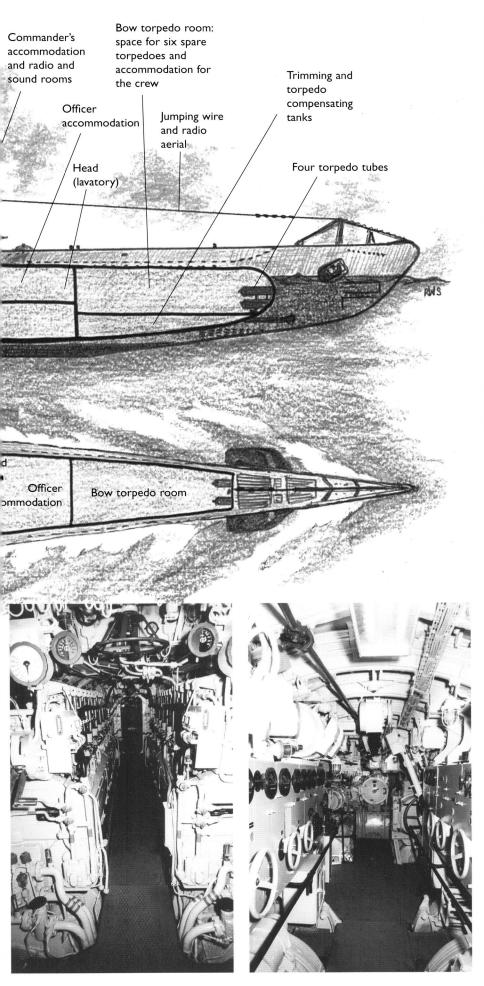

U177

U177 was a very long-range boat of Type IXD2, built at Deschimag AG Weser in Bremen. Wolfgang Hirschfeld, a U-boat radio operator and author of a famous war diary, said that he preferred bigger boats because they provided a higher state of comfort. However, at the time he was unlikely to have known that they also undertook exceedingly long tours. *U177* left Kiel for her maiden voyage to the South Atlantic on 17 September 1942, and then ran into Bordeaux on 22 January 1943. The next major voyage took the boat into the Indian Ocean for a period of 183 days with 60 or so men cramped inside a stinking and rocking hull. None of them could exercise properly and the vast majority hardly ever saw the sky.

WP=3, S=10, K=51

Far left: The diesel engine compartment of *U995*, photographed while the boat was being set up as a technical museum. These 3–4,000hp plants made so much noise that alarm bells could not be heard and a special flashing-light facility was installed in the engine room to show when the alarm was ringing.

Left: *U995* again, looking from the rear of the diesel compartment towards the single torpedo tube, with the emergency steering wheel tucked away sideways, toward the right. The tops of the electric motors are just visible above floor level and the later type of control panel can be seen towards the top. During the war, a torpedo was stored under the floor, in the space between the two motors.

Training

Very little would have been known about Hans Hellmann had his relatives or friends not left his fascinating handwritten diary in the U-Boot-Archiv. This document is of special interest because he was called up to join the Third Reich's first wartime emergency intake of naval officers. It provides, therefore, an insight into a period of exceptional turmoil, when a small core of a hundred or so U-boat commanders was suddenly enlarged to about 1,500. Official records tell us that Hellmann served as first watch officer aboard *U262* from April 1942 until June of the following the year, that he became a commander during a most difficult period in September 1943, and that he was murdered in Bremen on 3 March 1945, just two months and two days before the end of the war.

Hans Hellmann left school in March 1939 with the burning ambition to become a naval officer, but he had to complete a spell with the *Reichsarbeitsdienst*—the National Work Service—before being accepted by the military. So, he passed the summer months of that momentous year with a disciplined bunch of youngsters who made every effort to squeeze the maximum enjoyment out of the allocated tasks, and the bitter pill of compulsory work service was washed down with the thought that they were contributing something worthwhile to the nation.

September started with what Hellmann saw as the German reoccupation of its eastern territories, taken away after World War I to create a new Poland. Today, we usually see the invasion of Poland from the Allies' perspective, but Hellmann and his contemporaries would not have looked upon this in such a deeply derogatory manner. They would have known about the atrocities committed against those Germans who remained in the eastern regions when they became Polish, and consequently considered the reoccupation as liberation rather oppression. Hellmann spent his early years in Primkenau, only some 50km from the Polish frontier, so much of the dreadful goings-on would have filtered through to him by word of mouth rather than the official propaganda system, making the pain of brutality even worse.

The eastward thrust of the Blitzkrieg had hardly hit the headlines when, without much warning for the youngsters, Britain declared war on Germany, and it was not long before a large number from Hellmann's unit were called up early by the emergency mobilisation programme.

There never had been any forms nor special entry tests for the navy. Many of the modern military selection tests, now used by a multitude of nations, were then being pioneered by the SS, but the German navy remained firmly entrenched in its antiquated methods, which made it necessary to write a long detailed letter of application. Most of the applicants—those who met the stringent regulations and passed the appropriate medical—were invited to present themselves at one of the training centres for new recruits. Before the war, there were three of these: one in Kiel for the Baltic Command, another in Wilhelmshaven for the North Sea, and a third on the Island of Rügen specialising in officer candidates. The youngsters destined for this unit assembled in front of the railway station in Stralsund, to be taken by bus over the four-year-old dam to Germany's biggest island. This 2.5km road and rail connection had also been built by the Reichsarbeitsdienst to provide quick and easy access to the seaport of Sassnitz, a vital link in the train-ferry connection from Berlin to Sweden.

Still looking like a determined bunch of schoolboys with some experience in the Hitler Youth, the youngsters were driven at the double into what appeared to be meaningless tasks. The idea that you might dodge or shirk any of these was soon dispelled by a keen-eyed petty officer with a stop watch. Watching them run around the barrack block, he told them that they had slowed down while they were out of sight and they had better keep on going until they could maintain the same speed all the way. Grand Admiral Erich Raeder said that he found this stage of the proceedings so distasteful that he would have given up, had such an option been on the books. But he was brought up to cope with whatever adversities came his way and so gritted his teeth, put up with the harshness, and endured the first weeks of unimagined coarse austerity. Even prolonged spells with the Hitler Youth had not prepared the youngsters sufficiently for what they were expected to endure. Many years earlier, before the disasters of World War I, Germany

U178

The inscription starts, 'After lengthy construction and trials the swan is ready to go south ...' The men probably did not realise that the period from commissioning on 14 February to leaving Kiel on 8 September 1942 was not terribly long compared to the voyages the boat was going to undertake. Sailing several times into the Indian Ocean, and eventually going on as far as Penang and Singapore, *U178* remained at sea for 113, 122 and 180 days on three consecutive voyages. Living in the cramped confines of a wartime U-boat is a sacrifice the majority of people these days cannot even imagine, yet the men who did this regarded it as a necessity to help win the war.

WP=4, S=0, K=0

Above left: The exhausting training schedules were devised to take men to their limits, both physically and mentally. There was very little time for dealing with personal matters and long rests did not feature in the timetable, so it was necessary to catch up with lost sleep whenever the opportunity presented itself. A quick break during lessons was good for taking the odd nap.

Left: It is quite likely that Hans Hellmann is one of these recruits struggling through the snow. The carrying of the rifle had a twofold function: it gave the men an opportunity to handle such weapons and, at the same time, added a considerable burden to their activities.

had accepted into the officer corps dead wood with the appropriate social status. The National Socialists were determined that, despite the war emergency, the country was going to get the very best people to command the armed forces. Many of them had been in the Hitler Youth, today demonized as a depraved political organisation, although much of its indoctrination and pre-military training was not much different from that offered by the Scout and Guide movements of the Allied countries.

A good number of applicants were rejected during the first two days of training because they could not cope with the physical demands, and at the end of a fortnight or so numbers had been whittled down to a promising core of potential officer candidates. Despite the austere intensity of this initial training, many men said that it was exactly this harsh regime which helped them to survive the war and the extremely difficult period immediately after. The idea was to teach basic survival techniques and the necessary discipline to survive in the armed forces. It was given to every soldier, no matter what his aspirations or which service he wished to join.

On 30 November 1939, the initial training in Stralsund came to an end and those who survived made their way back to the railway station, wondering what was going to happen next. They knew that the majority was going aboard the old pre-World War I battleship *Schleswig-Holstein*, while a smaller proportion boarded its sister ship, the *Schlesien*. The administration and engineering officer candidates were due to join them later, after a spell at the Naval Officers' School in Mürwik (Flensburg).

Leaving at three o'clock in the morning meant that the trainees had to catch up with their hard-earned sleep the best they could while being jostled inside a rattling slow train, which did not arrive in Kiel until the late afternoon, when it was already on the verge of getting dark. The chaos of locating luggage from the baggage wagons did not last long, and the youngsters were pleased that a barge had been laid on to take them to their ship. That, at least, saved a long march with heavy kitbags or suitcases.

The *Schleswig-Holstein* seemed to be a maze of passages and ladders with an incredibly small amount of personal space, but the newcomers didn't get time to appreciate this fully. They were pleased that there was no opportunity to look around. Instead, hammocks were handed out and, being rather tired, it is highly unlikely that any of them heard the 'Silence on Board' whistle.

The first day on board was even stranger than the induction at Stralsund. None of them, not even the most proficient members with experience in the Hitler Youth, could cope with the stowing of

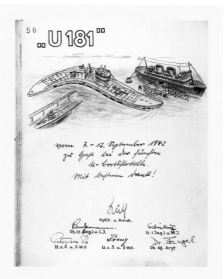

U181

This picture might suggest that *U181* had a small problem trying to get into Kiel harbour, although the commander executing the manoeuvre was one of the most famous. Wolfgang Lüth became one of only two U-boat men to be awarded the Knight's Cross with Oakleaves, Swords, and Diamonds —equivalent to winning the Knight's Cross four times. He died in a tragic mistake, accidentally shot by his own guard within the grounds of the Naval Officers' School a few days after the end of the war.

The other person to command *U181* was Kurt Freiwald, who had been adjutant to both grand admirals. He was chosen to take *U181* to the Far East in order to negotiate with Japanese authorities.

Note that the handwriting under the picture is in old German script, which was prohibited by the Allies after the war and has now gone virtually out of use.

WP=4 + 1 short patrol, S=0, K=0

hammocks. Following this seemingly impossible exercise, they discovered that there was hardly any space for turning round while washing. The normal chores of getting ready for the day became a real nightmare. Yet, despite the problems, no one came to blows and Hellmann even enjoyed being shown around the ship. In the afternoon, when everybody was introduced to their action stations, Hellmann found himself being shunted into a group responsible for one of the 150mm guns along the side of the ship. Following this, it seemed as if all the next days were taken up with cleaning, polishing, oiling or saluting everything in sight.

Then, unexpectedly, without a great deal of ceremony and almost without warning, everything came to a sudden grinding halt. The youngsters had long forgotten that there were such things as weekends and were pleased to discover that even the fast pace of the navy took a few hours off on Saturday afternoons and Sundays. Being free to do what they liked, the majority took the picket boat to the Hansa Pier, which was within convenient walking distance of town. This was the first occasion when they had free time to leave their posts, and it quickly became noticeable in the bars that there were good number of other ships in harbour. The battleships *Gneisenau* and *Admiral Scheer* and the cruisers *Königsberg* and *Köln* were all lying close by, as were a multitude of smaller boats and a number of prizes. As a

Above left: Hans Hellmann's year group running around the accommodation blocks during their initial training.

Left: Crew IX/39, meaning the men who joined the navy in November 1939, during exercises in Kiel. This is where Hellmann's side cheated by employing a group of eager, on-looking boys as reconnaissance scouts to tell them where the 'enemy' was hiding and the whole affair ended with a grand snowball fight.

consequence, the town was cloaked in a multitude of naval uniforms.

Training continued at a brisk pace, with the teaching of the roles the recruits had to perform depending on the condition of the ship—there were special roles for blackout, action stations, fire fighting, clean ship, closing watertight bulkheads and so forth. Then it was back to the guns again, and another dose of oil, more loading practice, more inspections and then the chance to manoeuvre a heavy cutter around the ship. This started out as a somewhat wet, uncomfortable and clumsy procedure with oars getting in the way, rather than moving the boat. Strangely enough, it was this punishing activity which later turned out to become the men's main recreation and wonderful excuse for getting away from it all. What could be a better way of avoiding the bark of petty officers and, at the same time, enjoy seeing the busy harbour from the closest of quarters?

The men had not yet become proficient at handling the cutter when *Schleswig-Holstein* left for a war patrol into the eastern Baltic with the task of checking on ships carrying possible contraband. Yet, despite this important role, there was no let-up in the training, and every opportunity was taken to practise various aspects of keeping the ship operational. In addition to this, the new recruits were expected to participate in a good number of tasks, such as standing on the quarterdeck for lifebuoy duty. The idea was that there should always be someone to throw lifebuoys in case men fell overboard. In fact, as you might expect, this rarely happened, and for most of the time lifebuoy duty amounted to no more than being out in the bitter cold for a four-hour stretch. It appeared as if the order 'Buoy Overboard' was only given at times when the recruits were settling in some enjoyably easy pastime. Since the ship was not going anywhere special and the officers on the bridge had plenty of time, they would stop for the cutters to be lowered at the double while breathless youngsters manned the oars to race through the wildest of weather to recover the floating buoy. This was not the only comfort thief on board. There were even more hated, free-time-robbing occupations, such as fetching food from the galleys and washing the utensils afterwards.

For much of the time the newcomers, who had not yet been promoted to cadets, didn't even know what was going on around them and had to concentrate on a heavy cocktail of lessons. On one occasion they noticed a lighthouse sliding past outside the bullseyes and guessed that they were approaching a harbour.

Although their instruction, lectures and practising took priority over virtually everything, there were opportunities to participate in what the *Schleswig-Holstein*

was doing, and a deliberate effort was made to inform them about the history of the areas they visited. For example, while in Danzig, the men were taken on a tour of the Westerplatte, a spit of narrow land held by Poles for several days after the rest of the nation had capitulated. There they saw the remains of fortifications that had stood up to a barrage from *Schleswig-Holstein*'s guns at the start of the Polish campaign. Stepping on deck that Saturday morning of 16 December 1939, for the usual hammock inspection, everybody realised that it had turned exceedingly cold overnight. The way to keep warm was to get those cutters out for a chaotic, but good-natured race before being allowed the freedom to explore this bustling metropolis of East Prussia.

The contrast when they headed west, through fiercely cutting winds, from the illuminated freedom of the eastern Baltic to a blacked-out and war-prepared Kiel, made more of an impression on the youngsters than the arrangements for Christmas.

As with so many other institutions, the navy closed down for the festivities, with large numbers—particularly of married men —leaving for home. There was no respite, however, for new recruits who had to remain on board, but they could look forward to the luxury of three days off—with Christmas Eve falling on a Sunday, it meant that everybody gained an extra long holiday.

Nevertheless many of the youngsters found this to be an especially hard period. As it was the first time that many of them had

U213

U213 was an unusual type with a number of mineshafts immediately aft of the conning tower. The commander, Oblt zur See Amelung von Varendorff, learned his trade in *U47* under Kplt Günther Prien and was on board when this boat penetrated the defences of the Royal Navy's anchorage at Scapa Flow to sink the battleship *Royal Oak*. He had a reputation for being a wild character, but his luck did not hold out. He took *U213* on only three patrols before being sunk with all hands on 31 July 1942. The boat's second voyage was out of the ordinary inasmuch as it dropped an agent in Fundy Bay near Saint John (New Brunswick) in Canada.

WP=3, S=0, K=50

Above left: Maintenance work on the 37mm quick-firing deck gun with the man wearing both a lifejacket and safety harness.

Far left: Crew IX/39 wearing field grey naval infantry uniforms during their initial training. Many of these activities looked rather innocuous, but anybody having gone through the process will know that they sap energy from the body, making difficult to concentrate and to aim guns accurately.

been away from their parents for any length of time, they missed the atmosphere of home. To make matters worse, the military field post system failed to deliver Christmas mail for many of them. Some were lucky to have heard from home and received welcome gifts, but the others had to bear the pain of loneliness and homesickness made worse by the feeling of being forgotten.

Yet, despite these natural feelings of depression, the recruits of the German navy showed they were the same as any other young men in such circumstances. They may have had a hard training programme, but they knew how to celebrate, and the days of Christmas passed very quickly.

The last revellers did not return until 07:30 on 8 January 1940, cutting things rather fine for an 08:00 departure through the Kiel Canal. The fresh water in the canal had not stood up as well as the sea to the low temperatures, and the armoured bows of the *Schleswig-Holstein* were called upon to act as icebreakers for the more delicate commercial traffic and smaller units of the Kriegsmarine. Negotiating such a thin ribbon of water was something new, and many men took the opportunity to watch the goings-on. The locking process and then passing under the amazingly high bridges brought out especially large numbers.

It was around midday that the *Schleswig-Holstein* passed the Colonial Girls' School in Rendsburg, where tradition had it that warships must sound their horns and dip their flags. Whether this interrupted lessons or not, the greeting was always acknowledged by masses of waving and cheering girls.

Another consolation was that artillery practice was cancelled, because warships were prohibited from elevating or rotating their guns while in the canal, but this was a short-lived joy. Those recruits who hadn't learned it by now soon realised that their time was always filled by some sweat-provoking activity or other, and there were few opportunities for quiet rests. In any case, the news wasn't that welcome because the youngsters had the rather interesting carrot hanging in front of them that they could fire the guns before the end of the month, if they were proficient enough by then.

By the time—19:00 hours—*Schleswig-Holstein* approached the locks in Brunsbüttel on the Elbe estuary, her decks resembled a pleasure cruiser there were so many people out in the darkness to watch the illuminated locking process once more. This time the spectators got more than they bargained for. One of the trusses from the tugs got caught in the propellers, and was wound in at an alarming rate until the spectacle came to stunning halt. Five hours later, *Schleswig-Holstein* was eventually docked while a good number red faces scurried about the still immobile ship. Not only was this inconvenient for those on board, but the massive size of the vessel ensured that nothing else was going to use that lock until something was done about the constriction around the screw. During the first signs of daylight, some early risers watched a diver go down, but they were not allowed out for too long since their superiors demanded that they turned their attention to the subject of communications and so they attended a lecture by the radio officer, Oblt zur See Bernhard Zurmühlen (who would be killed in the North Atlantic during 1943 as commander of *U600*).

The rope around the propeller caused a number of U-boats to become blocked-in as well, and the recruits' had to acquire sufficient hammocks to accommodate the U-boat crews aboard the battleship, because the confines of the small boats were unbearably cold. The visitors' spartan comfort didn't last long. Air raid sirens howled their frightening tune and, racing up on deck, Hans Hellmann found himself thrown into the bitterness of a cold night with the immediate prospect of ending his career before it even started. Lights were extinguished, the guns were manned and high-intensity beams swept the skies, making barrage balloons appear like strange, hovering UFOs. It seemed unreal and a long time to wait for nothing to happen—the aircraft weren't interested in the well-armed ships by the locks and continued further inland to deposit their bombs on some other unsuspecting, and probably less well defended, target.

Making fast on buoy A4 in Kiel was followed by the satisfying experience of watching their engineering and administrative colleagues from the initial training join them aboard. Hans Hellmann and his mates realised they were no longer raw recruits, and that there were others who could not cope with that arduous task of tying hammocks, something which had already become second nature for the old lags. It was quite a boost in confidence for the youngsters to discover that they were not the only ones who got lost among the maze of passages and banged their heads in the exceedingly constricted spaces.

The cold weather with intermittent snowstorms continued, as did the intensive training. The next excitement did not come until 20 January when *Schleswig-Holstein* was given the mission to escort some ships through the Small Belt. Blinding snow made it difficult to determine the exact route through minefields and even worse visibility prevented the battleship from going back into the Kiel Förde. It became embarrassingly obvious that there was no need to drop anchor while waiting: the ship

U214

U214 was an unusual minelayer of Type VIID, of which only half a dozen were built. The boat had four commanders, sailed on 12 voyages, sank three ships and damaged two more, operated off Freetown in Africa, in the western Atlantic, in the Caribbean and laid mines off Plymouth, South Devon (England).

This is a remarkably varied career, especially when one considers that more than 650 U-boats never got within shooting distance of a target.

U214's luck ran out on 26 July 1944, when she was depth-charged and sunk with all hands by the frigate HMS *Cooke*.

WP=11 + 1 short patrol, S=0, K=48

had attached itself firmly to a sandbank. Hellmann and his mates would hardly have noticed, had it not been for the commotion of rattling engines trying to pull free, but no further progress was made, not even with the help from a powerful tug. Both drinking and washing water were pumped out and then an array of six tugs attempted to pull the heavy giant. Even with all engines straining at full power, nothing much happened, other than that *Schleswig-Holstein* developed an irritating list. Nine hours later, after an intensive effort, a great deal of speculation from recruits and swearing from the ship's crew, *Schleswig-Holstein* made fast on buoy A4 in Kiel. All dry docks were fully occupied, giving ample fuel for rumours that they were going through the canal to Wilhelmshaven.

Weather-wise it was getting noticeably warmer, but there were ample places where salty water still looked like a white rockery, meaning there was no hope of a run ashore because it was too dangerous for small pickets boats to be out. The recruits watched the heavy cruiser *Admiral Hipper* being brought out of dry dock and guessed

that they were destined for a spell in there. They hoped they would get some free time ashore, but rather than have an easier time, training seemed to intensify, and shutting down parts of the ship meant that the men had to cope with additional chores. Since it was no longer possible to wash or use the heads (toilets), everybody had to undertake a rather long walk to facilities on land, without being given extra time to do so— causing training to continue at a more frenzied pace than before. Getting to the lavatories, or heads, was indeed a major problem, but applicants with weak bladders had already been weeded out.

Hellmann was far more concerned with the distance between the dry dock and town, on the opposite side of the water. The few hours for their occasional run ashore had suddenly been shortened considerably. Instead of being able to walk into an abundance of bars, it was now necessary to take a tram. Getting back late at night in overcrowded conditions meant that the youngsters had to hang onto the outside. Even then, it still involved a good jog at fast pace to get back before the leave period

Above left: A brief pause in training. Much of the early training was land-based where men wore the naval field grey uniform.

Left: Hans Hellmann, the author of the diary on which this account is based. He was born on 8 March 1921 near the Polish border, became a U-boat commander and was murdered in Bremen just before the end of the war by an irate husband, who felt he had become too intimate with his wife. Naval authorities took a strong stand against men having affairs with married women, and before the war the punishment was instant dismissal. However, other authorities within the Third Reich did not consider such conduct too bad. Indeed, one such disgraced naval officer, Reinhard Heydrich, took a commission in the SS.

expired. Of course, being in dry dock gave the cadets an opportunity of examining their ship from the outside and peer at the massive crack in the hull. In a way it was quite comforting to know that huge holes could be torn in the metal plating without water pouring in to sink the ship.

Lying next to the dry dock was the sail training ship *Albert Leo Schlageter*. Had it not been for the war, the cadets would have been sailing in this type of magnificent 'rag steamer', as they were known in the German navy. There were enough older men itching to go aboard to re-live their younger years and after some wheeling and dealing the cadets were shown the intricacies of sailing. Hellmann felt somewhat uncomfortable knowing that he was part of the first officer crew which did not have the opportunity of training aboard one of these magnificent ships. It was even more frustrating when the older lags related how they had visited warm tropical countries as part of their prewar education process.

There were faint hopes of the training easing, but petty officers were similar to Rottweilers and didn't let up. Those selected to conduct officer training knew full well that one day they might be commanded by the men who they were training and there was no way they wished to work for prunes. Therefore, the cadets got the best on offer. With the restrictions of the dry dock, they merely switched to land-based infantry training, to take their charges into the local parks, sports grounds and through slush-filled streets. Hellmann was pleased that despite the more attractive nautical training, he and his fellows had not forgotten what they had learned during their initial training at Stralsund. There was even time for a number of war games among the hills behind the houses, but Hellmann's group found an excellent opportunity of cheating. Finding a small army of boys as onlookers, they quickly took advantage, engaged the eager children and sent them off to search out the 'enemy'. Following that unofficial intelligence, it was an easy matter to creep up on the opposition through waist high snow. The day ended not with a mock battle, but with a snowball fight of immense proportions in which even the petty officer task masters joined in.

On 10 February, Hellmann found himself woken especially early to prepare for undocking. The plan was to have sufficient men standing by to prevent the ship from scraping along the edge of the dry dock or possibly colliding with other obstacles. At this critical stage, and without much warning, the engines gave out. Instead of steam being forced into them, it escaped up the funnels. Consequently a large number of hawsers were thrown considerable distances to prevent disaster. Sadly, there was no relief for the cadets,

who were looking forward to going to sea and shooting the guns for real. Instead a number of ominous scraping sounds indicated that they were destined to remain in dry dock.

This time, the cadets were ordered aboard the accommodation ship *Monte Olivia*, where they were nearer washrooms and heads, but found their new quarters uncomfortably cold. Engines were not running and there were no facilities for external heating, meaning that several layers of clothing had to be worn just to be reasonably comfortable. On one occasion, Hellmann found that his towel had frozen so stiff that it could be stood upright on its own without falling over. A quick glance at all ships of those times will reveal that open bridges featured in navies all around the world and the military was quite happy for its soldiers to endure the discomforts thrown up by the elements. Despite the cold, training continued unabated and infantry exercises on land took on a new light, since they provided an opportunity of working up some warmth. Hellmann found that one major problem with the naval education system was that new topics were started before the youngsters had time to digest what they had just learnt. But then, no one got into an officer's training programme without a finishing certificate from a recognised Gymnasium or grammar school, which indicated that they had the ability to learn fast.

Left: Two instructors with their charges during initial training. The recruits are wearing white denim clothing, which was popular both on land and for general work aboard ships. The trucks on which they are sitting were quite common at the time. They were used on building sites, quarries and other places where heavy loads had to be moved. The tracks were often laid temporarily along roads to overcome the problem of carrying heavy loads over soft ground or rough cobblestones. Heavy loads were still moved by horses and carts until some time after World War II. Lorries composed only a tiny fraction of the traffic on roads, many of which were unsurfaced tracks—even the more busy highways were covered with bumpy cobblestones. The vast majority of modern, tarmac surfaces did not appear on the continent of Europe until long after the war.

U217

'Having sunshine in the heart' didn't prolong the life of Kptlt Kurt Reichenbach-Klinke and his crew of 49. All of them went down with this Type VIID when it was attacked by aircraft from the carrier USS *Bogue* during its third operational voyage. However the first two watch officers had started their commander training by then and survived the war. Max Kruschka commanded *U621* and Friedrich-August Gréus *U737* and *U716*.

WP=3, S=0, K=50

Left: The naval barracks in Wilhelmshaven around the time when Hitler came to power. 'Lord Muck', lounging on the chair and being serenaded, claimed he was too hard worked to clean his locker properly prior to an inspection, so his mates are giving him a hand to make sure that the offending piece of furniture is spotless. Some punishment was called for and coping with a wet wooden locker was not terribly congenial because the offender could not lock his clothes away until it had dried out again. Consequently he was confined to barracks for a brief period while the rest of the 'charmen' had a run in town.

It was the end of the first week aboard the *Monte Olivia*, on 17 February 1940, that Hellmann wrote:

'*... in the evening we were told about the Altmark incident. We heard from all parts of the world that English forces broke neutrality by invading Norwegian territorial waters. This piece of piracy resulted in the boarding of the German steamer* Altmark *and the murder of several German sailors.*'

As time progressed it became evident that the enforced period in dock was presenting not only the educators but also the cadets with ample frustration. Having to practise things like manning the guns without being able to fire them was annoying. So was navigation. Having mastered the complexity of the sextants, for example, many cadets found that they could find their position reasonably well, but they hardly had the opportunity of trying this intricate process aboard a rolling ship, where it was more difficult to align the sights.

It was 12 March when the *Schleswig-Holstein* was undocked. The icy winter had long been forgotten and the first signs of spring were showing on land but the salty water still held a good number of ice floes, somewhere between half and three quarters of a metre thick. Trials at sea were quick and decisive, but hardly affected the cadets who continued to be put through their usual paces. Following this, frustrating gremlins continued to play their part. Having put to sea for gunnery trials everybody discovered that the fog was not going to lift for them to see the targets. Conditions improved later in the day, when the cadets were pushed through the punishing schedule of keeping the guns shooting at a fast rate. During the afternoon, when the grim weather made it look like evening, searchlights were brought in to continue with the all-important artillery training. Easter celebrations went by the wayside and the cadets bathed in sweat to complete their punishing schedules.

Torpedo shooting was practised in Eckerförde Bay, home of the Torpedo Inspectorate, because a large number of specially modified 'eels' were required, as well as a flotilla of small boats to retrieve them at the end of their run. The dominant trail of oil and bubbles was supplemented with a lamp so that the exercises could continue in the dark, but this process did not get very far when *Schleswig-Holstein* turned and made back to Kiel at fast speed. Although none of the cadets knew it yet, they were going to miss out on a considerable amount of sleep to get the ship ready for the invasion of Norway and Denmark. The commander, Kpt zur See Günther Horstmann, called the men onto

U225

This standard Type VIIC sailed on two patrols under Oblt zur See Wolfgang Leimkühler, sank one ship and damaged four more in a short operational life of 10 weeks and 2 days—exactly half as long as its working-up period. The boat left the 5th Flotilla in Kiel on 5 December 1942 to spend Christmas out in the bitter weather of the Atlantic and then made for Brest where the boat was repaired and refuelled from 8 January 1943 until 2 February. Thirteen days later, when a Liberator from No 120 Squadron RAF attacked, U225 was sunk with the entire complement of 46.

WP=2, S=0, K=46

Above: Keeping the 105mm quick-firing deck gun in working order. These weapons were cumbersome and there were many complaints that conditions were only rarely good enough to use them. Kptlt Herbert Schultze of U48, the most successful boat of the war, said that it was often criminal to order the gun crew on deck and such action caused more problems than it was worth. The maintenance of these large guns was quite complicated. They had an unusually large number of over 40 grease nipples, but still seized up exceedingly quickly.

Left: Many naval quarters on land were only a little less cramped than conditions on board ships. During training periods, each man was usually allocated a cupboard which had to be kept locked—the reason being that one should not tempt others to steal. The men are wearing white working denims over blue naval shirts with the large 'Nelson' collar.

the quarterdeck to inform them of their new role. Wondering whether they would remain on board or not, the cadets participated in loading to find out that they were nothing more than gofers for the more experienced men. A good number were ordered off, but the ship's crew was too short-handed and some were due to sail with the old battleship to Korsor in Denmark.

Once again gremlins decided otherwise. Running aground, all the men could do was to wave while the rest of the fleet sailed past. The cadets quickly guessed from the engine noises and the swirling of water that someone had done it again. Sadly, such incidents are not good news for those at the end of the pecking order, who had to get the cutters out to carry the heavy anchors far away and then drop them without sinking their small boats. Despite pulling on the chains with the help of a tug, it was soon clear that *Schleswig-Holstein* would not be going to war and the cadets could concentrate on their examinations instead.

Hans Hellmann discovered a satisfyingly confident feeling on 20 April, when a good number of wine bottles appeared to celebrate the Führer's birthday and promotion to *Fähnrich zur See* (Probationary Officer Candidate or Midshipman).

Sailing to Gotenhafen, there was a formal dinner before the cadets left for a most welcome few days of home leave in a splendid-looking uniform. Before leaving it was made quite clear that the last six months should not be looked upon as having launched them on a naval officer's career, but have given them the qualification to start becoming one. The education process at the Naval Officers' School in Mürwik (Flensburg) was going to be especially difficult because everybody was going to miss out on that all-important aspect of going to sea and experiencing the worst enemy they were likely to face, the rough natural elements. This was, undoubtedly, one of the most significant detrimental factors affecting the efficiency of U-boats. The vast majority of boats in the punishing restlessness of the Atlantic appeared to be faced with the lethargic reactions of men suffering from severe seasickness.

It may be worth reflecting on the type of schooling Hellmann and his contemporaries had experienced. They started their day at 8:00am and would have had a short as well as a longer breakfast

U251

Although this boat has been recorded as having had three commanders, only two them were in charge of the boat. The third, Oblt zur See Joachim Sauerbier, was a passenger to Norway when the boat was sunk by aircraft to the south of Göteborg. This happened just two weeks before the end of the war, meaning that the majority of the men killed with Sauerbier had been in the thick of action in cold Arctic waters for the most difficult period of the war since 18 April 1942 and almost survived. Both commanders survived. The second was Oblt zur See Franz Säck and the first, Korvkpt Heinrich 'Tüte' Timm, was later made leader of a midget weapons unit. He became a prisoner of war and was not discharged until April 1948.

WP=9 + 2 transport patrols, S=0, K=39

Above left: The light cruiser *Köln* during a spell of rough weather when the new recruits seek out railings to do what comes naturally in unstable conditions. Seasickness was indeed a major force to be reckoned with and a considerable number of U-boats in the Atlantic were probably lost because the men inside were too ill to react properly to threats from aircraft and escorts.

Left: Just being able to row a cutter was not good enough and there were numerous official and unofficial races.

break, when they ate sandwiches brought from home, before going home for lunch and homework at about 13:00. Lessons were dominated by German, Mathematics, Geography, History and one or two foreign languages. It is quite likely that the majority also studied Latin in depth and, during their later years, a little Science. Although some form of Physical Education would have slotted into the programme, it is highly unlikely that Games formed an official part of the timetable. There would have been very little or no technical education and virtually no hands-on practical work. So, Hellmann's generation left school with little or no practical experience of the type of work they were going to face in the future.

At the age of 18, these youngsters might have achieved high academic standards, but they would hardly have been well-informed about what was going on in the world around them. The subjects pumped into them at the Naval Officers' School was supposed to focus on this deficiency by teaching the basics for running ships. Yet, much of the time was devoted to theory rather than trying things out practically and the system concentrated on keeping uniforms clean rather than mucking-in and trying things out. In September 1941, when the majority of youngsters from Hellmann's year group emerged as fully fledged naval officers, Germany's navy was so small that there was little choice other than to join the U-boat arm. This, however, was not seen as a drawback—rather as an excellent opportunity for early responsibility.

The general scenario of war had changed considerably by the time Hellmann's group headed east to Pillau to start their U-boat watch officer training with the 26th U-Flotilla. Three months earlier, Germany had invaded Russia and the Eastern Front demanded that urgent war supplies be given priority on the

Above right: Remains of Polish fortifications on the Westerplatte by Danzig were frequently visited for people to admire how the small garrison there stood up against the might of the German onslaught, after the rest of the country had capitulated. The Westerplatte was a long and narrow spit of land on the seaward side of Danzig. Taken away from Germany after World War I, it became a heavily fortified part of the new Republic of Poland. Although some action by the Polish forces was futile, such as attacking tanks with lancers on horseback, many Germans appreciated the audacious bravery of its soldiers.

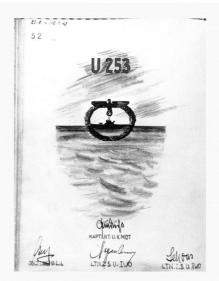

U253

U253 was commissioned by Kptlt Adolf Friedrichs on 21 October 1941 and left the 5th Flotilla in Kiel for its first operational voyage on 12 September 1942, having spent almost a year getting ready for war. On the 25 September, that is less than two weeks later, the boat was sunk on a mine to the south of Jan Mayen Island. There were no survivors.

WP=1, S=0, K=46

Left: *U1233* negotiating the Kiel Canal with one of the high railway bridges in the background. Many commanders with the special canal 'ticket' for passing through on their own, still took a pilot because that gave them some time off to lie on their bunk instead of standing on the top of the conning tower for up to nine hours. Three different pilots were usually required for different stages of the waterway.

railways. Consequently the young naval officers frequently found themselves being shunted into sidings, meaning that the journey took much longer than expected. The education in Pillau was very much a mishmash of theory and practical, often with part of the day spent in a classroom and the rest at sea trying out what had been learnt. The advantage with this was that the small school boats were often back in port before the bars closed and there was ample time to discuss the day's proceedings over a glass of wine or beer. What happened next depended on each individual's marks. Those like Hellmann, who were quick off the mark, found themselves pushed into an operational U-boat, while others followed a slightly different route.

Although it was early March 1942 when Hellmann stepped out of a train in Bremen, the air was still definitely chilled from the preceding harsh winter and greatcoats with scarves and gloves were still the order of the day. Reporting to Kptlt Günter Schiebusch at the ship yard of Bremer Vulkan, Hellmann arrived just in time to witness the launching of *U262*. One day short of five weeks later, he stood on deck while the flag was hoisted for the first time and he officially became the boat's first first watch officer—a proud moment and quite an achievement, but not necessarily for the better. Three years earlier he was still sitting on a school bench and now, suddenly, this quick-witted and eager youngster carried a burden of expectation almost as heavy as the boat itself.

At least in Kptlt Günter Schiebusch he had the advantage of having a well-experienced commander, who had been in the thick of things since before the beginning of the war. However, although Schiebusch was indeed a remarkable character, he proved not to be the type who turned out to be a successful U-boat commander. Having been aboard the pocket battleship *Admiral Graf Spee*, he had made his way from internment in South America back to Germany, to serve aboard the heavy cruiser *Prinz Eugen* until December 1940, when he embarked upon the intense programme of submarine training. At this stage he showed sufficient promise to be promoted to command *U252* with very little U-boat experience, but ended up in hospital just a few weeks after the commissioning in October 1941. Consequently this command was passed on to Kptlt Kai Lerchen and in March 1942 Schiebusch took over the brand-new *U262*. His new boat was commissioned exactly one day after *U252* was sunk with all hands.

A general murmuring of displeasure among the crew of *U262* was loud and persistent enough to be heard on land, and it was not long before Schiebusch was relieved of his command to be made first officer aboard the destroyer *Hans Lody*

(Z10). From there he became first officer aboard *Theodor Riedel* (Z6) and then he occupied a number of land-based positions. It is easy to condemn such a person, but a good number of high aces also broke under the immense strain and some of them acknowledged that the U-boat arm was too harsh in the way it treated its officers. One highly successful commander, 'Ajax' Bleichrodt, said that Admiral Dönitz demanded too much of his men and he should have incorporated a safety valve into the system so that people were not driven into the one-way dead ends in which many finished up.

On 20 October 1942, *U262* was taken over by Kptlt Heinz Franke, an ordinary person who hardly created a stir in the crowd, but one with an ability to remain calm under fire. He was one of about 600 applicants who joined the navy in 1936, the year of the Olympic Games in Berlin and Garmisch-Partenkirchen. About 100 of these applicants were whittled out during the first two days because they could not meet the challenging physical pace. A few of the more enthusiastic youngsters were told to join a sport club and come back in a year's time, while the remaining men were given naval uniforms to start their basic training as seamen. At this stage the group was made up of the following applicants: 367 deck officers, 66 engineering officers, 21 medical officers, 36 weapons officers, 28 administration officers and 10 construction officials, making a total of 528 youngsters between the ages of 17 and 21 years. This meant that the vast majority came direct from grammar school with virtually no experience of the world far beyond the classroom. (Hellmann's crew X/39 was made as follows: 361 deck officers, 101 engineering officers, 70 medical officers, 44 weapons officers, 28 administration officers, 34 construction officers, making a total of 638.)

Following three months of initial military training, the group was split into three for basic professional training. Deck and medical officer applicants were distributed among the sail training ship *Gorch Fock*, the sailing schooner *Duhnen* and the old battleship *Schlesien*—Germany had launched only the one 'White Swan of the Baltic', and it was too small to accommodate the entire contingent. Engineering and administration officer applicants were sent for workshop training at the Naval Academy in Mürwik, while weapons officers spent the next three months at the Naval Arsenal in Kiel. Although the youngsters were now well on the way to becoming naval officers, there were still fatalities and numbers were whittled further. One person, for example, found that he had no head for heights and could not cope with the rigging, meaning there was no alternative other than a

U255

This standard Type VIIC features in a good many history books because it spent a great deal of its operational life exploring the cold Polar Sea, at one stage operating with a Blohm und Voss flying boat to search out possible convoy routes among the icebergs of the north. The boat was commissioned by Kptlt Reinhard Reche on 29 November 1941 and then sailed on 21 patrols. The last voyages were undertaken in shallow water from French bases in the Bay of Biscay, sailing in April 1945 from St Nazaire, to La Pallice and back again, before making for Norway. However, the war ended while the boat was still at sea and it surrendered in Loch Alsh near the Isle of Skye in Scotland.

WP=21 including transit/ transport patrols, S=--, K=--

Above left: Engineering cadets at the Naval Officers' School in Mürwik. There was more emphasis on hard physical training than practical instruction and, as can be seen here, some workshop activities were of a spectators' nature, rather than getting ones hands dirty.

Below left: Issuing Dräger lungs by the escape training tank. This submarine escape apparatus doubled up as a lifejacket and could also be used as a respirator in emergencies. Breathing with it was not easy, as it required a considerable effort to force air in and out.

discharge. Although the cadets aboard *Gorch Fock* considered themselves as the cream of the navy, they were in for a harder time than the rest and there were no special privileges. In fact, very much the opposite happened. During the opening ceremony of the Olympic Games at the Kiel Yacht Club, they were not even allowed on deck and had to watch the proceedings by taking turns to peep through the bullseyes. The exceedingly limited space below decks made this quite difficult and the almost unbearable temperatures of those summer months added further to the discomfort.

The temperature quickly changed for the cooler when *Gorch Fock* headed north through the Baltic, to sail around the north of Skagen and then on to the Royal Navy's academy at Dartmouth in Devon. There the youngsters, who still had not yet been promoted to cadets, were surprised and horrified to discover that their presence was shunned by the military. British naval officers were not allowed to talk to the Germans while they were shown around the imposing naval school and drinking water from taps on land, which was usually free in every port of the world, was charged for. Many of the youngsters could not understand the cold shoulder, but guessed that it had something do with the success back home, and the British government wanted to make the point that it did not agree with National Socialism. It was suggested by *Gorch Fock's* commander that the visit should be cut short, but this request was refused by the Supreme Naval Command in Berlin and the sailors just had

to turn a blind eye to the bristling hostility from British officialdom. At least this was displaced, to some extent, by a most warm welcome from the local civilian population, who gave every indication of being eager to make contact with the foreigners.

September 1936 saw the officer crew or year group back in Germany for promotion to sea cadet and distribution aboard the light cruiser *Emden* and the battleships *Schleswig-Holstein* and *Schlesien* for seven-month-long tours into foreign waters. It was only the medical officers who missed out on finding their sea-legs by having to indulge in further practical studies in naval hospitals. As was often the case during those turbulent prewar years, the foreign tours were not as straightforward as might be imagined, and the men aboard the *Emden* found themselves participating in the Spanish Civil War to help rescue German civilians. The majority were delighted when the ties to this commitment were lifted and the ship headed further south.

On 1 May 1937 the whole crew met once more in Germany for promotion to *Fähnrich zur See*. Once again they paraded, while the commanding officer addressed the assembled company—but, as had been the case on several previous occasions, there was no microphone and the majority could not hear what was being said. This was followed by another 10–11 months of courses at the Naval School in Mürwik and concluded with the customary written and practical examinations. To make sure that the youngsters had not forgotten anything

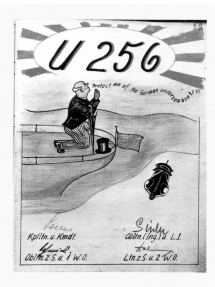

U256

U256 had a most remarkable career in the North Atlantic, and was used a Flak trap in the Bay of Biscay. After that the boat was thrown against the D-Day invasion supply routes. It shot down several aircraft but paid for its success by being damaged beyond use. Its crew managed to bring their boat back into Brest, where it was classed as 'unserviceable scrap'. The twin problems of American troops reaching the outskirts of the town and a number of severe air raids with 'Tallboy' bombs blasting holes through the U-boat bunker's roof, did not prevent the wreck from being repaired and *U256* provided its last gram of service by taking the commander of the 9th U-boat Flotilla, Korvkpt Heinrich Lehmann-Willenbrock, and a number of men to Norway, where the boat was finally decommissioned.

WP=5 + 1 transport patrol, S=--, K=--

Above left: A meeting with *U160* under Kptlt Gerhard Lassen.

Left: The top of the diving tank at the U-boat school. Although a number of men ended up in U-boats without an introductory training period, the majority were put through an induction course which involved practising escaping from sunken U-boats.

they were sent to sea once more for practical training aboard ships. July 1938 started with promotion to *Oberfähnrich zur See* and this coincided with a period of resting on laurels. At least it appeared as such to many, who had got used to the intense pace of the previous months. On 1 October 1938, when the surviving cadets had been in the navy for 30 months, they were promoted to *Leutnant zur See* (Sub-Lieutenant).

Heinz Franke had the opportunity of going home on leave for a few days before taking up an appointment as anti-aircraft officer aboard the *Gneisenau*, where he remained for almost two years until October 1940, when he embarked upon a programme of submarine training. Following this, he served as first watch officer aboard *U84* under Horst Uphoff. His training to become a commander lasted less than two months and then he took over *U148* from Oblt zur See Eberhard Mohr. This was a tiny coastal boat of 500–600 tons with no more than about 22 men on board and was used for training in the Baltic. Although somewhat limiting, it did give him the feel of what it was like to be at sea on his own.

Franke had hardly found his feet when, without much warning, he was told to pack his bags and make his way to Narvik in northern Norway to take over *U262*, a much larger Type VIIC with a partly experienced crew. Hans Hellmann was pleased to greet his new boss and quickly found that he got on much better with him. Together they experienced the bitterness of the North Atlantic before running into La Pallice in France. The boat's third voyage from there saw a momentous, if unsuccessful, undertaking—they crawled under the thick ice of the Cabot Straight in Canada with a view to attempting a rescue of escaped prisoners of war.

By the time Hellmann reported to the 24th U-Flotilla in the far eastern Baltic for his commander training, he could have been said to be a well-experienced U-boat officer with first-hand knowledge of the horrors of the Atlantic. The next stage of his training lasted for a bare three months from June to the end of August 1943. On 4 September he made his way to the small Flender Werft in Lübeck to commission *U903*, a brand new Type VIIC, earmarked for training duties. This gave him the opportunity of trying out what he had learned, without being faced with a deadly enemy.

His next command, *U733*, was also used for training in the eastern Baltic. Actually it was sunk on 8 August 1943 in the approaches of Gotenhafen harbour as a result of a collision with the Patrol Boat *V313*, but was raised a week later, to be repaired and then commissioned a second

time by Hans Hellmann.

Around this time the records lost touch with Hellmann, but we do know that he made his way to Bremen to be murdered by a jealous husband who did not like Hellmann having an intimate relationship with his wife.

It is a sad reflection of European leadership that so many energetic youngsters like Hellmann, from all sides, spent all their 'adult' life after school doing nothing more than fighting.

Above: U-boat history books deal with crew and sometimes mention dock workers, but the vast army of other essential supporters are often forgotten. This is the ferry man, 'Rucks Willi' (Willi the Puller) because he pulled his boat using a lever hooked over a cable. Everybody in 21st (Training) U-Flotilla at Pillau knew him. No matter how bad the weather, he was always there, taking men from their base to the high life in town and back again.

U261

Despite this most impressive picture with grandiose inscription, *U261* was sunk to the northwest of Lewis in the Outer Hebrides by a Whitley bomber from No 58 Squadron, RAF, exactly one week after leaving the 5th Flotilla in Kiel. The commander, Kptlt Hans Lange, was no newcomer to submarines. He never served as watch officer, but did command *U61* for best part of a year before taking on this new boat. He should not be confused with Harald Lange, who commanded *U505* when it was captured by United States forces in June 1944. Hans Lange was born in Bremen on 29 May 1915 and joined the Kriegsmarine during the year of its foundation in 1935.

WP=1, S=0, K=43

Left: Fähnrich zur See Johannes Kühne from Brandenburg who later served as first and second watch officer aboard *U387* and as commander of *U2371*. This is what the men looked like when they left their training to take up a position in the navy. However, the Minesweeper Badge above the National Sports' Badge indicates that Kühne has already seen some action. The ribbon through the top buttonhole indicates that he has also been awarded the Iron Cross Second Class. The star on the sleeve shows that he is a sea or deck officer.

Life in U-boats

Although the operational side of submarines dominated the crew to such an extent that it took priority over everything, much of the life on board was governed by boring domestic chores, rather than coldly calculated battle orders. Walter Hartmann discovered this soon after he had volunteered to join *U162* under Kptlt Jürgen Wattenberg. In addition to being a torpedo mechanic, Hartmann was appointed batman for the first watch officer and orderly for the officers' mess. This had the advantage that he did not have to participate in other domestic chores in the rear torpedo compartment, where his hammock was located, and allowed him to wander around, picking up snippets of news from other people's conversation.

Yet, whether he was washing dishes for officers or men didn't make much difference. The mess was the same, although the quantity of crockery was rapidly reduced by depth charges and bad weather. In any case, washing was not high on the list of priorities, and at sea the dishes received only a rub over with warm seawater from the cooling system in the engine room. There was no detergent or soap and the only aid, other than a large dixie, was a rag of questionable appearance. Hartmann said that U-boat hygiene can hardly be imagined, and it is not until one has experienced a regimen such as this that one fully appreciates the high value of living on land.

Those early training days in the Baltic were not typical, inasmuch that the boat was usually back in port for the evenings, so there was often time for a wash and brush up before seeking out a local bar. However, this had the disadvantage that the majority of men lost their sea-feet and had to get accustomed to the pitching and rolling anew each day. This was not too much of a problem at first because the boat spent a considerable period submerged, trying out a vast variety of diving exercises. These were approached most cautiously, with men on tenterhooks, expecting the boat to crack up when they heard the ferocious noises caused by the squeezing of the hull by the intense water pressure. It was Hartmann's duty to be ready to open a vent in the rear diving tanks as soon as the alarm bells shrilled, and to report immediately to the central control room. Not only did these tasks have to be performed quickly, but they had to be done automatically. Once operational, if you were woken from deep sleep you had to cope instantly with the machinery, even in total darkness.

Everything went well and the tests quickly passed on to the next stage, where Hartmann was responsible for the emergency steering wheel. This was folded away sideways, but could be swung out into the centre of the rear compartment. There was a primitive indicator showing the angle of the rudder, but no compass, so directions had to be passed from the central control room by telephone or word of mouth. This was not terribly easy, especially when noisy diesel engines hindered the relaying of orders.

Next, having mastered the controls, everybody was chased out through the hatch in the diesel compartment, to climb up the outside of the conning tower and down into the control room. It was essential that everybody should be able to perform this simple action quickly and efficiently, without clambering about on the ladder or hesitating at the bottom before clearing the spot for another person. It was achieved by gripping the rails on both sides and sending your body into a controlled fall, checking the speed with the handhold on the rails. Torpedo mechanics, who were unlikely to be on deck during an alarm dive, were given a few seconds extra, but the lookouts were not allowed to rest until the entire diving procedure could be carried out in less than 36 seconds—an incredibly exacting piece of highly co-ordinated team work was required to achieve this.

Diving time was measured from the ringing of the bells to there being several of metres of water above the top of the conning tower—so it was essential for everybody to get below and for the duty officer or commander to close the hatch before it was engulfed in water. The engineering officer, standing at the bottom of the ladder, keeping one eye on the hatch above him and another on the diving controls, had to be prepared to countermand the diving procedure in case things went wrong and the boat dropped away before the hatch was shut.

That is not to say that the torpedo mixers had an easy time. It wasn't long

Right: Although the higher ranks of *U18* had mess tables, they were just as cramped as the 'Lords' in the bow compartment and teamwork was very much the operative word to get food passed along. These tables were erected along the passage in the middle of the boat, making it virtually impossible for anyone else to move from one end to the other, meaning there was no way of getting to the head or lavatory during meal times.

U333

U333's first commander, Kptlt Peter Erich Cremer (better known as 'Ali'), was descended from British aristocracy. Among other things he has the unique distinction of having collided with enemy ships on three separate occasions, but each time managed to bring his badly damaged boat home again. He is also responsible for accidentally sinking the German freighter-cum-supply ship *Spreewald*, but that did not prevent him from being awarded the Knight's Cross. At the end of the war, he became chief of Admiral Dönitz's last guard, while the admiral headed the remains of the German government in the Naval School at Mürwik. *U333* sailed on 12 patrols from 27 December 1941 until 31 July 1944 when it was sunk near the Isles of Scilly by Squid forward-firing mortars from the sloop HMS *Starling* and the frigate HMS *Loch Killin*.

WP=11, S=0, K=46

before the boat was filled with practice 'eels' for shooting at moving targets. This week-long ordeal involved a considerable physical effort as they were reloading virtually non-stop all day long. These early exercises did not always pass without casualties. It was almost exactly a year later, on 12 November 1942, when the first watch officer, Oblt zur See Horst Hepp, who had been promoted to command *U272* by then, was sunk during a collision with *U634* while on torpedo trials. The boat was quickly raised again, but several men lost their lives and it took a while before the machinery could be repaired.

U162 eventually passed the Agru-Front tests to go back to Kiel for finishing-off work. At the same time, the majority of men were allowed a few days of home leave. Since it was necessary to empty the boat before leaving, a good number of sausages, tins of honey, coffee beans and other delicacies got lost, vanishing into private kitbags rather than be returned to the quartermaster's stores. Although kitbags were the only sensible means of carrying anything into a U-boat, they were so awkward to handle that the majority of men preferred suitcases for long journeys. For Hartmann and his colleagues, this was the first opportunity they had had to go home since having joined the navy some ten months earlier, so it was necessary to go into town first, to buy a suitcase to carry the loot.

Hartmann made the rather poignant point that his sister was, coincidentally, also on leave at the same time and those few brief days together was the last time the family met for 25 long years. The reason for the separation was that Hartmann's home town of Leipzig came under Russian jurisdiction after the war, making it virtually impossible to travel there from the west. It seems strange that so much Allied propaganda referred to Europe being liberated, but the conditions imposed by the victorious Allies—particularly the Russians—were in some cases as bad as those imposed by the National Socialists. Sadly, when the victors write the history books, there are few mentions of offences against basic human rights, committed by the Allies after the war.

It was early February 1942 when the men of *U162* were back in Kiel to provision the boat for its first operational cruise. This involved taking on board 23 torpedoes as well as mountains of stores. It was necessary to strap a couple of torpedoes into the central passageway of both stern and bow compartments, and then fit another set of floor plates over the top. This left just sufficient room for men to stand up and the crates stowed on top of this false floor served as seats. Both Type IX and VII had two lavatories or heads. However, it was common to use one of them as a larder, hence the almost 50 men on board shared one small facility in the rear compartment.

Above left: *U31*, a Type VIIA. Although men often took advantage of eating on the upper or promenade deck, there was not much more space than in the interior and such luxury was hardly possible at sea, where boats often had to dive exceedingly fast.

Above: Putting the 'Wintergarten' or 'conservatory' to good use.

Right: The lower bunks of *U103*, an ocean-going boat of Type IXB. Although men were sometimes at action stations for long periods or working on lengthy repairs, overcoming boredom was very much a problem, especially on long voyages. Ample reading matter and records were taken along and some men even provided live entertainment. However, even reading became a major problem when boats were forced to remain submerged for long periods, because often there was not enough power to keep the lighting system running and men would then spend most of their time in gloomy conditions. The rails on the sides of the bunks were necessary to prevent the occupants falling out during rough seas.

Right: *U621* showing the multitude of hams and sausages hanging about the interior. Although food was distributed throughout the boat, men were not allowed to help themselves and could only consume what was provided by the cook. This rule was, of course, relaxed once the boat was on its way home and personal items for nibbling were sometimes handed out. Dr Klaus Törpisch of *U594* said that oil vapour condensed on the food and after a few days at sea everything tasted and smelt the same.

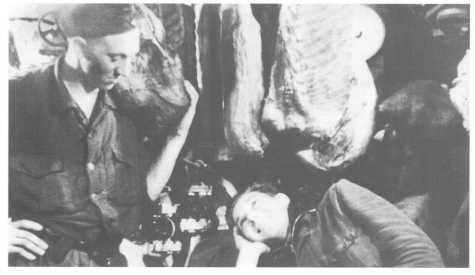

And getting into it was no easy matter, since a couple of hammocks with fresh bread were strung in front of the door.

Following a final run ashore, with a good meal and a few bottles of wine in a good restaurant, both Hartmann and his friend Bruno staggered back over a slippery covering of ice. The following day *U162* nosed out behind the icebreaker *Wotan* to negotiate the ice-blocked Kiel Canal. This was no easy matter and could well have led to the destruction of the bows. To prevent this a massive and rather heavy bow cap was added to the front to protect the delicate outer doors of the torpedo tubes. The cap was removed again on arrival at Heligoland, where a diver also examined the propellers for possible damage from the thick ice, which stretched far out into the salty waters of the Elbe estuary.

Training for the crew and tests for the machinery continued unabated while the U-boat pushed its way northwards at the most economical cruising speed of six knots. This was achieved by driving the boat with one propeller and using the other shaft as a generator to charge the batteries. This went exceedingly well and it quickly became apparent that the machinery was in considerably better fettle than the men. Virtually everybody on board was seasick, making the daily tasks awfully hard going. The navy could not afford to carry passengers, so the men were expected to perform their duties no matter how badly they felt, and for most of the time they were only allowed a few brief minutes to be physically sick. Once they had thrown up the contents of their stomachs, they were expected to be back at their posts. To make matters worse, there were no opportunities to lean over the side railings, the navy did not supply bags for such purpose and receptacles were not always at hand. Seasickness presented a major obstacle for the operational efficiency of any new boat and the smell added a most appalling air to the stuffy interior.

Even torpedo mechanics, who might have thought that they had a cushy option, found that there was a great deal of maintenance to be carried out— frequently accompanied by an outpouring of richly elaborate vocabulary, of the sort usually not found in dictionaries. The torpedoes in the tubes could not be pulled out for their regular service unless the two torpedoes lying immediately behind them were rolled out of the way first. This meant that everybody in the compartment had to move into the extremities. There was no hope of the off-duty watch dozing in their bunks because these had to be folded up. Such work was so demanding that the torpedo mixers in the rear compartment commuted to the bows to help out there and vice versa when the other end required attention.

Jürgen Wattenberg, the commander, had served as communications officer aboard the ill-fated pocket battleship *Admiral Graf Spee* since 1938 and so had enough experience to know how to ease his men through the discomforts of the North Atlantic. Knowing there was little that he could do until they found their seafeet, he alternated the routine between a hectic programme of practising and moments to take it easy. Meals were virtually always consumed deep in the depths, where the men could sit quietly without having to worry about the boat or anticipate the vibrant shrill of alarm bells. Although these huge, vicious clangers were designed to wake the dead, they could hardly be heard in the diesel compartment, where the deafening thumping of the engines drowned out every other sound. This problem was overcome by a most ingenious system of flashing lights, which made it obvious that alarm bells were ringing and that the engines had to be shut down.

The only way of relieving the monotony of the daily chores and getting some fresh air was to ask permission to climb up to the top of the conning tower, but even this could not always be given because the threat from air attacks was too great in some areas. Instead the men had content themselves with lurking inside the conning tower control room, behind the surface rudder position, where they were allowed to smoke as long as the hatch remained open. In *U162*, someone even rigged up an ingenious electric cigarette lighter so that matches were not needed.

Hartmann had hardly acquainted himself with his chores and duties when he was called forward by the duty officer and told to have a go at steering the boat. Instead of the large manual wheel, for which he was responsible in the rear compartment, he had to get used to the electrical controls by pressing one of two buttons to move the rudder left or right. In rough conditions it was virtually impossible to sit upright, so the control box was fitted with two grips to steady yourself and the contacts were then immediately below the palms of the hands, meaning the operator could clutch the supports while also pressing the appropriate button. This was not as easy as it sounds and often a counter-movement was necessary to prevent the boat from swinging too far. The lookouts could amuse themselves by watching the zigzag course until the new helmsman got the hang of the process and steered a straight line.

The smaller sea-going Type VII-boats did not have enough room inside the conning tower for a steering position, so these boats were controlled from the central control room. Helmsmen in all types of boats were also responsible for the relaying of orders to the engine room and this

U337

Oblt zur See Kurt Ruwiedel started this page with, 'We are aroused by this visitors' book the same way as a bull is excited by a red rag. Many thanks. We would like to offer our hand.' He left the 5th Flotilla on Christmas Eve of 1942 and then vanished into the vastness of the Atlantic. The boat was believed to have gone down somewhere near Newfoundland, but the exact cause and date of the sinking have never been ascertained, although the loss has been put down as 15 January 1943. One wonders whether the men departed on Thursday, 24 December to get away from the emotional bustle of Christmas or whether an order prevented the men from enjoying the festivities in port. Strangely U377 'vanished' in similarly mysterious circumstances on the same day exactly one year later.

WP=1, S=0, K=47

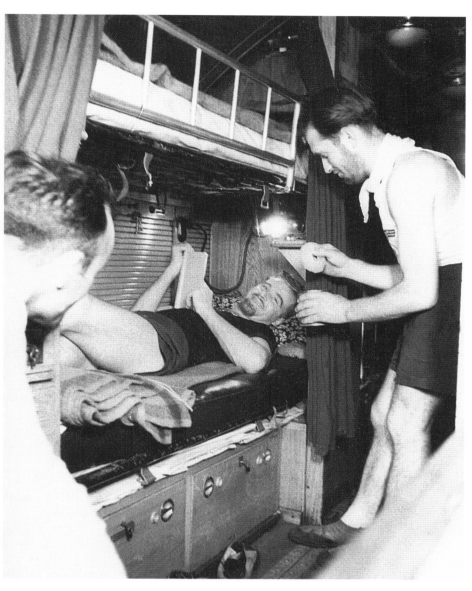

U356

U356 (under Kptlt Georg Wallas until 2 December 1941 and Oblt zur See Günther Ruppelt from 3 December) sailed on three patrols, sank three ships and damaged one more, making it one of the more successful U-boats. It left the 5th U-Flotilla in Kiel on September 1942 and was sunk by Canadian ships on 27 December of that same year, while hunting some 400 miles north of the Azores. All 46 men on board were killed. This standard Type VIIC boat was built at the small yard of Flensburger Schiffbau, which was brought into submarine construction after the beginning of the war.

WP=2, S=0, K=46

sometimes added a new dimension to the entertainment on board. It was not uncommon to have the boat going round in circles because one engine was running faster than the other and appropriate instructions given to induce the trainee to make the right adjustments. Of course, every boat had its proficient 'action stations' operators for every task, but it was essential to train more men to relieve these people. Therefore, many commanders took many opportunities for allowing other men to learn new tasks.

Teething problems with the machinery were being sorted out and the men were adjusting to the constant restlessness of the sea when they were confronted with a storm of unexpected ferocity. The majority felt somewhat pleased that they weathered this without too much trouble, although the men in the torpedo compartments had an exceptionally uncomfortable time when they were thrown against iron bulkheads. Bruises and cuts were common enough not to be reported and there were no serious injuries, but soon afterwards it was discovered that the hydroplanes had

suffered even worse than the men. These had bashed so hard into the waves that something must have got bent and was preventing their usual free and easy movement. It was one of those agonising decisions and in the end both commander and engineering officer decided it might be best to make for port.

This had hardly been digested when far worse was discovered. The torpedo tubes had flooded themselves, suggesting that the outer doors were no longer watertight. Indeed opening the outer doors in the bows was impossible and a closer external examination was called for. This indicated that fairings in front of the watertight doors were hanging loose. After a great deal of discussion, it was decided that they had to removed. Safety lines were rigged and the rear tanks flooded, while the tanks in bows were blown, to lift the tubes high up in the water so that men could clamber down into the icy wetness of the North Atlantic to remove the outer doors. This was a most nerve-tingling situation indeed, and the majority of the crew was busy praying that they would not be discovered by an aircraft. For the best part of

Above left: The very long-range boats of Type IXD2 had almost luxurious accommodation compared with the smaller types. Wolfgang Hirschfeld (radio operator of *U109* and *U234*, and—postwar—an author) said, in his famous diary, that he chose to join larger boats because conditions were so much more bearable. This shows the officers' quarters of *U178*.

Left: Ernst Beinert and Walter Schöckel of *U103* relaxing on the metal floor plates of the engine room. Both men appear to be wearing leather trousers and Walter (on the right) his sports vest.

Right: Siegfried Lüdden, as IWO of *U129*, who later became commander of *U188* and was burned to death during a fire aboard the accommodation ship *Daressalam* in January 1945. This clearly shows the use of an open-air head on the upper deck. The term 'head' comes from the days when the officers lived in the stern of wooden ships and men went to the bows or 'head' to relieve themselves. This picture shows that some World War II submariners were provided with even inferior lavatories to those aboard the old wooden walls. Paper was usually not supplied and one must bear in mind that the boat was pitching and rolling, while chugging along at about ten knots, making the balancing act on this throne rather an arduous matter.

Below: *U1169* on one of those warm, calm days in the far eastern Baltic, where nothing was likely to interrupt a few peaceful minutes on the upper deck.

ten hours, the boat lay motionless on the surface, unable to dive, while the biggest and strongest men were chosen to get on with the sawing. They were kept alive by a constant supply of grog, made with rum and hot water. Wattenberg was so impressed by this performance that these men were the first to be awarded Iron Crosses.

Hartmann was dozing in his hammock strung in front of the torpedo tubes when the telephone rang. Being able to reach it without getting up, he grabbed the handset, expecting to hear that it was time to empty the gash buckets. Instead he was told to report to the radio room. Two of the operators there had been taken ill and an extra set of hands was required. There was no way that he could find his way around the masses of delicate equipment, but he was given a quick lesson in handling the secret coding machine and then given a pile of meaningless text to convert into readable messages. As consolation he found a tiny work surface for the heavy machine and was pleased that he did not have balance it on his knees.

Table space was a major problem in both the bow and stern compartments—so much so, that there were no flat surfaces for

even the most elementary of jobs, such as eating. The men had to sit wherever there was space, often on the floor, and balance plates on their knees. The food was not bad, although it tended to get somewhat monotonous once the fresh ingredients ran out, but there were hardly ever any shortages and usually there was a plentiful supply of everything. However, coping with meals which required knife and fork was not easy and men preferred it when things had been cut into mouth-sized portions before they wedged themselves into position.

Hartmann said that much of the food became covered in a layer of mould and this had to be scraped off before it was prepared or eaten, but this never seemed to have hurt anyone and there never were any cases of men suffering from the ill effects of poor hygiene. In fact, the hygienic aspects of eating were best not thought about. Often one sitting would eat from the utensils used by the previous, without washing them first. On the other hand, if the boat was on its to way to France, rather than going on to America, the food was declared 'free' meaning the men could eat whatever they liked whenever it took their fancy. Earlier, each man was issued with a number of personal delicacies, but otherwise was only allowed to eat the food which was provided and could not help himself from the vast stocks in the boat.

Crossing the Bay of Biscay at night to avoid the ever increasingly dangerous threat from aircraft, *U162* met an escort on the seaward side of the minefield protecting Lorient, to run into France with a single success pennant fluttering from the extended periscope. The men had good reasons for their high spirits, although the damage prevented them from reaching their primary objective, that of hunting on the American side of the Atlantic. They had seen the ocean at its worst, attacked a number of targets and survived. The reception was fantastic, with military band and everything well prepared. Even mail from home was ready, waiting to be picked up. Sadly, the arrival in Lorient did not provide any instant relief for Hartmann, who remained on board together with the other 'mixers' to unload the remaining torpedoes. It was late afternoon before they arrived in the barracks for a hot shower, a clean uniform and then were able to enjoy the high life of a riotous party. The first such celebration was usually on the house, with an unlimited supply of free beer flowing as long as men could stand up to drink it.

The fact that this was the first time in five weeks that he had taken off his clothes, hit him especially hard and made Hartmann realise how cold it had been aboard the U-boat, where everybody lived constantly inside a number of heavy layers

U403

This standard Type VIIC worked the convoy routes of the North Atlantic from March 1942 until August 1943, sinking two ships. This was not a great deal of success when one considers the amount of resources which were put in to get it to sea. Yet, *U403* did better than 650 other U-boats which never got within shooting range of the enemy. This performance of sinking two ships in almost one and half years hardly adds up to the image of the 'deadly hunter' which has been portrayed so often by the media. The first commander, Kptlt Heinz-Ehlert Clausen, survived the war by being promoted to Chief of the Trials Group Sultan but the second, Kptlt Karl-Franz Heine, was killed together with the rest of the crew, when *U403* was depth charged by a Wellington from No 697 Squadron, RAF and a Hudson from No 200 Squadron, RAF off Dakar on 18 August 1943.

WP=10, S=0, K=50

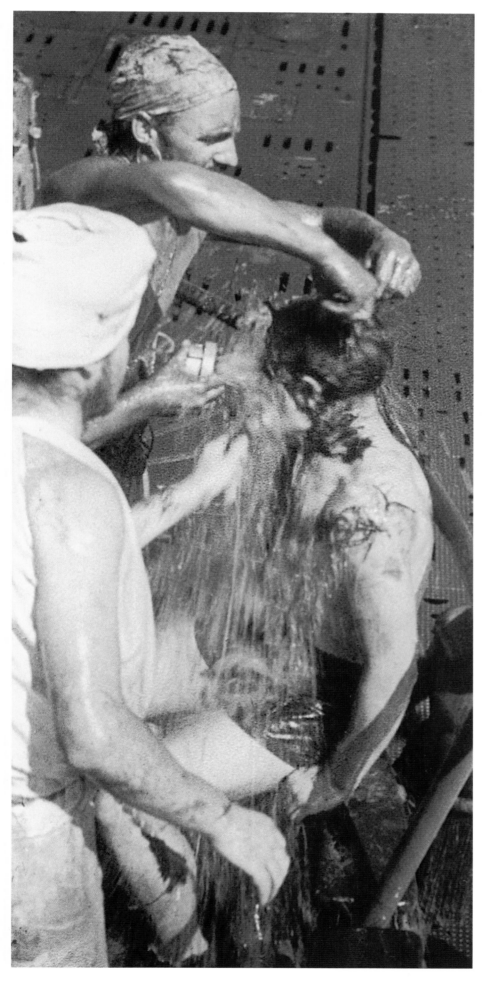

U404

Korvkpt Otto von Bülow, *U404*'s first commander, became a Knight of the Iron Cross twice, meaning that he wore the much coveted cross together with the small silver Oakleaves. In September 1943 he was promoted to command the 23rd U-boat Flotilla in Danzig. This flotilla specialised in teaching new commanders the intricacies of shooting torpedoes. When he was finally driven from his base by advancing Russian armies, von Bülow made his way west to Hamburg where he took command of *U2545*, a new Type XXI. It would appear that this posting does not feature in many official documents, but has been recorded in the diary of submarine designer, Christoph Aschmoneit.

WP=7, S=0, K=50

Left, Far left and following pages: Crossing the line (Equator) celebrations were always an excuse to go wild and the cleaning of dirty sailors from the north took on a barbaric nature. Had prisoners of war been treated in a similar manner, the perpetrators would no doubt have faced a court martial once back home in Germany.

U405

Korvkpt Rolf-Heinrich Hopman spelt his name the English way with only one 'n' at the end. He commissioned *U405* on 17 September 1941 and remained in command for two years of bitter patrols, most of them into Polar waters. On 1 November 1943, the boat came to a most dramatic end by being rammed by the United States destroyer *Borie*. It would appear that the two became locked together and American sailors then gunned down about 30 Germans as they tried to escape from their sinking boat. Realising what was happening on the outside, the rest of the crew then remained inside, deciding to go down with their boat when it was dislodged from the destroyer's bows. Scuttling charges had been set and these detonations ensured that the remaining men died inside their iron coffin.

WP=11 + 2 transit patrols, S=0, K=49

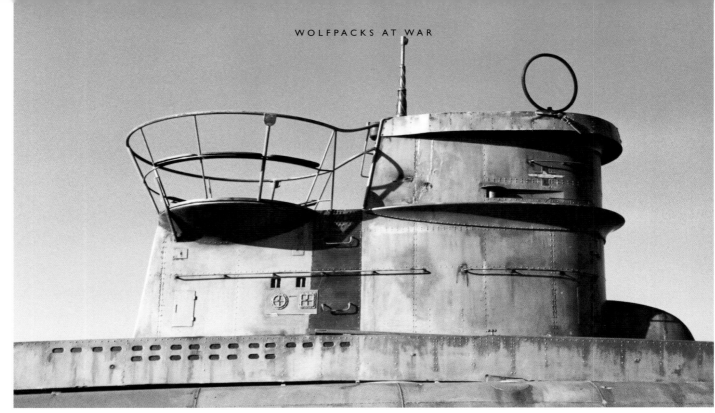

Right: *U52* being refuelled in Lorient during April 1941. Boats had inlet connectors for fuel, lubricating oils, drinking water and washing water as well as heating connections for attaching steam hoses. Since boats were usually filled up under supervision of the engineering officer, the caps could be well hidden below the upper deck. However, boats also had emergency ventilation and tank blowing connections for non-specialists rescue workers and therefore these inlets were clearly marked with universal symbols ...

Above: ...both the emergency ventilation inlet and tank blowing connection are marked with a cross inside a circle and a cross inside a square by the side of the ladder leading up to the 'Wintergarden'. These were not painted on, but welded proud, so that they could be found by touch. This shows a remarkable model of a Type VII conning tower on display at Bletchley Park in Milton Keynes (England). The circular radio direction finder is not authentic. It seems likely that this has been copied from the one on the museum boat at Laboe near Kiel, where the original one, shown in photographs in this book, was stolen and has since been replaced by a mock-up.

Right: Men cleaning the 105mm quick-firing gun barrel aboard *U178* under Kpt zur See Hans Ibbeken. The majority of photographs tend to show U-boat men lounging around rather than working. The reason being that this was often the only time they had for taking pictures.

to keep warm. With an average temperature around 10°C and no additional heaters, the majority of men found themselves all the time in cool and damp surroundings where everything, including Hartmann's camera, developed a layer of dense mould.

Having recovered from the ordeal of celebrating long into the night, the men took to exploring the town of Lorient rather than allowing themselves to be overcome by the services on offer within the naval base. The locals were friendly, offering a wide variety of delicacies and drinks to tempt sailors with money to spend. It was almost the end of March 1942, meaning spring had already made a considerable impression on the Biscay coast, which contrasted considerably to the letters from home, describing the harshness of the winter with an abundance of snow.

Getting away from the navy was not that easy: there were a good number of chores such as cleaning out the boat and attending the obligatory medical. This was brought to a sudden and unexpected climax by the confirmation that the radio mechanic, who had been taken ill earlier, was suffering from the highly infectious disease, tuberculosis. Luckily none of the others was infected. This potential killer helped to render the seven cases of lice insignificant, although the men tended to take a poor view of anyone harbouring such creatures. This time the suspected cause, a young midshipman, had already departed for further training elsewhere. On reflection, Hartmann realised how lucky they all had been and how little was required to throw the entire operation into more gruesome dimensions.

In a way the men were astonished at the speed with which the boat was heaved out of the water inside the massive bunker, to be shunted aboard a many-wheeled railway buggy and into a dry pen. The pace of the repair work was rapid and it seemed no time at all before new crates started arriving for the next voyage. The fact that helmets for the tropics were being issued suggested that *U162* was going somewhere hot, but otherwise the men had no idea what was afoot. It was Good Friday 1942 when the boat was ready to put to sea, but the periscopes developed a mysterious fault and required the attention of an expert, postponing departure. Such 'tragic' cases of machinery malfunctioning occurred most frequently when there were orders to leave on a Friday. Since this tradition of not leaving port on Fridays was older than everybody in the navy, the majority of higher officers turned a blind eye, but throughout the Third Reich there were a few isolated cases of men being landed in trouble by over-anxious desk warriors for refusing to put out to sea on a Friday.

Departure was quite a problem. It was thought that the French Resistance had countless observers along the coast in constant contact with the Allies to report departing U-boats, but this was not the case. Britain got to know about boats at sea through the radio signals they themselves sent back to the land-based operations room. When they reported that they had crossed the Bay of Biscay, it was possible for the Royal Navy to work out the approximate latitude such signals were coming from and thus could make a calculated guess as to where the U-boat was heading. During this period of the war, the plan was to leave at such a time that the far side of the minefield could be reached shortly before nightfall, to provide ample darkness for getting far away from the coast before daylight could make detection by aircraft easier. In fact, cruising on the surface during the day was virtually impossible and the rising sun usually drove the boats into the cellar.

One of the torpedo mixers from the bow compartment had been sent away for further training as petty officer and so Hartmann was moved forwards to the more demanding position in the front, but it didn't make much difference. Life there was just as uncomfortable as in the stern, although there were more men with whom one could exchange the odd word. The most interesting point was the steadily increasing temperature both inside and outside. It was no longer necessary to wear several layers just to keep warm in bed and there were ample opportunities to lie on the upper deck with warm water washing over you. This certainly was not only a good way of keeping cool, but also most welcome for washing. The saltwater soap was not terribly effective and hardly removed oily grime, but it did help to wash away the superfluous sweat and make people feel fresher.

Wattenberg took advantage of eggs rotting rather quickly in the warm, moist air by using them for artillery practice. One crate at a time was thrown overboard, to be sunk by gunfire before it passed out of sight. This took place at such a leisurely rate that the galley hatch was opened to bring the ammunition up. The hatches along the main pressure hull were usually kept closed because it was far too easy for waves to wash down into the boat. This meant that during action heavy ammunition had to be carried up the inside of the conning tower, through the main hatch and then be brought down the outside ladders to upper deck level. The majority of these shells were stored inside sealed metal containers with a lever to break them open. This storage system was so efficient that the shells removed from wrecks at the turn of the century, more than 50 years after manufacture, were still in

U407

U407 was another one of those little-known boats. It sailed on a number of operational patrols, most of them in the Mediterranean, sinking four ships and damaging three more. Oblt zur See Ernst-Ulrich Brüller, who signed this page, became Chief of the First Submarine Training Division in February 1944 and thus survived the war. This, incidentally had nothing to do with training, but was a cover name for a personnel pool of men available to take up vacancies aboard U-boats. The second commander, Oblt zur See Hubertus Korndörfer, who first commanded *U139* and later *U3537*, also survived the war. Even the third and last, Oblt zur See Hans Kolbus, was among 48 survivors picked up when *U407* was sunk on 19 September 1944 by RN destroyers *Garland*, *Terpsichore* and *Troubridge*.

WP=12, S=48, K=6

Right: It is rather difficult to make out what these two men are doing. Surely they are not passing a container with heavy 88mm shell? Whatever, the rough weather harness being worn by the man in the foreground is of special interest. These were usually donned only at times when conditions were too rough for men to be standing around with cameras and, therefore, do not feature in many pictures. These men are wearing the harness together with a lifejacket. The photograph was taken in 1942 aboard *U572* under Oblt zur See Heinz Hirsacker. A court martial would find him guilty of cowardice in the face of the enemy and he was executed by firing squad on 24 April 1943.

Right: *U564* under Reinhard Suhren, who gained the Knight's Cross as 1WO of *U48*, was the most successful boat of World War II. What is going on in this photograph? It is tempting to suggest that the men are bringing a torpedo from the external upper deck container into the stern compartment, but that would not account for the inflatable in the background nor for the clutter around the torpedo resting on its cradle. This standard Type VIIC boat made several journeys as far as the Caribbean and was then refuelled in mid-Atlantic. It seems highly likely that this picture was taken during one of those occasions. It shows how precarious work on the upper deck was and why the men had to wear stout safety harnesses.

useable condition. However, these sealed metal containers were not universal and some U-boats carried their ammunition in waxed cardboard tubes. Small quantities of cartridges were stored in pressure-resistant containers under the upper deck, although the main magazine was located underneath the radio room.

For most of the time on board, none of the crew knew exactly where they were, although men passing through the central control room could easily stop off to glance at the chart. It was hardly secret, but just something the men usually did not bother with. On this occasion, many started taking an interest in that thin pencil line, especially as it encroached ever closer to the Equator. Only Wattenberg had been so far south, and despite there being no real old lags aboard, the opportunity was grabbed for the usual crossing of the line ceremony (see photographs of such an event on pages 52–55). By that time the men knew that they were heading for Trinidad and Barbados. The water temperature was 28°C and it was at least 35°C inside the boat, producing a horrid damp greenhouse air, which drained the men of energy. A vast quantity of lemonade essence had been taken along, but there was a shortage of fresh water, meaning that it was not possible to slurp it down in the quantities the men would have liked. There was a fresh-water generator or still aboard, but this required electricity and was only switched on in dire emergencies.

Uniforms by now consisted of light games shorts, sailing shoes and the obligatory shirt for those out on the upper deck. Yet despite the light attire, it was still necessary to wear a small rag or towel around the neck to wipe off excess sweat. Jock straps had been issued in reasonable quantities back in France and these were now coming into their own, despite the majority of men not having worn such garments before.

Action was not long in coming, but the first target turned out to be sailing ship. Sinking it was not easy. It left a multitude of crates and barrels floating in the water including one with a turkey perched on top. This had hardly been rescued when a couple of pigs were spotted, to be picked up as well. It was not a humanitarian event, but a way to supplement the monotonous died of tinned food. There was a butcher on board and all three provided an attractive variation to the menu.

MAN OVERBOARD

It seems highly probable that the number of people who died as a result of being washed overboard from U-boats has never been fully investigated, but a rough estimate suggests that the total could reach well over 1,000. Details were not always recorded in logs and, sadly, there were times when men just vanished amidst the confusion of serious action during a dark night, not to be missed until sometime later when it was too late. One such case is mentioned briefly in the chapter dealing with the voyage from Lorient to Norway in August 1944 (see pages 106–113).

One must bear in mind that crew members were more likely to be washed off the deck or conning tower during exceptionally rough weather when hostile natural elements added considerable problems to recovery attempts. The German navy was certainly not flippant about such occurrences. Ample precautions to prevent such disasters were taken and recovering lifebelts from the water formed a crucial part of the education process. Large surface ships usually had a man on duty at the stern doing nothing but standing there on lifebelt duty (see page 26). However, one only needs to look at photographs of submarines in mild Atlantic swells to realise

U412

U412 was commissioned by Kptlt Walther Jahrmärker on 29 April 1942 and left the 5th Flotilla in Kiel six months later, on 17 October. Five days later the boat was caught in the beam of a Leigh Light from a Wellington bomber of No 179 Squadron, RAF. *U412* was sunk by four well-placed depth charges. There were no survivors. Jahrmärker joined the navy in 1935, the year that Hitler repudiated the Treaty of Versailles, reintroduced national conscription and initiated new defence laws.

WP=1, S=0, K=48

Left: With such a small number of men inside each U-boat, it was necessary for many of them to become efficient jacks-of-all-trades. It is surprising how much heavy steel on submarines was torn loose at sea, and small welding jobs were part of the maintenance routine, especially for long-range boats.

how easy it was to be washed overboard. To prevent such accidents, submariners wore a relatively comfortable mountaineering type of harness with carabiner hooks to chain themselves to the conning tower. Yet, despite having been made from substantial materials, some of these broke under the immense strains of keeping lookout in Atlantic gales. There was hardly any railing along the upper deck, but the stout jumping wires running from the top of the conning tower to the stern and bows were designed to be used as fasteners for safety lines and allowed men to move along the deck without too many obstructions.

Although a vast number incidents of being washed overboard ended in disaster, there were a number of cases where men were recovered under the most incredible circumstances. One such incident occurred aboard *U382*, when Oberbootsmaat Sepp Leinenbach was swept into the teeth of an Atlantic hurricane. He clambered down from the conning tower to repair some serious damage from a depth charge attack, when his safety harness snapped. Screams from the lookouts were followed by the commander yelling his orders down to the central control room while the small dot of a head quickly vanished from sight among the mountainous seas. The waves

and wind were so noisy that it was difficult to hear, even when men were shouting at the tops of their voices and this added to the slight delay of turning the boat round. Bearing in mind that *U382* was pitching and rolling on waves much higher than an average family house, the problem of finding such a small object as a person was exceedingly difficult. The boat could be in one trough, while Leinenbach could have been close by in another without one being able to see the other.

Ten minutes passed, twenty minutes, thirty minutes. No sight of Leinenbach. The commander climbed down into the central control room, stood by the navigator, Stabsoberbootsmann W. Jüngler, and asked, 'Exactly where did he go overboard?' With a stop watch in his hand, he had written down the course changes and times. Despite men hardly being able to stand up and a number of injuries due having been thrown against bulkheads or even sharper projections, the commander told the men to keep looking. There was no way they were giving up a colleague. It was 50 minutes after having been swept overboard when Leinenbach was sighted and a number of men risked their lives to clamber down onto the upper deck to recover him from what had almost become his grave.

Above: Although many periscopes were made from high quality stainless steel, they still needed a considerable amount of maintenance. The main tube had to be kept greased and lenses often required cleaning and drying out. Condensation was theoretically prevented from forming on the inside by inserting a moisture absorbing cartridge. The active chemical in this was coloured with cobalt chloride, a blue indicator which turned reddish pink when damp. It was then placed on the hot plate of the galley to dry out and could later be reused.

Right: *U178* with signal lamp in action. Commanders were loath to use the radio in case their position was found by radio direction finders; they often fell back on old-fashioned communication methods. The rod in the foreground is an extendable aerial. Initially these had to be wound up and down by hand, but by the time the war started the majority of boats were fitted with electric mechanisms.

Not all man overboard incidents were as dramatic as Leinenbach's experience, but a number were used to fuel the rather harsh gallows sense of humour necessary to remain sane in the appalling conditions. For example, in April 1942, the engineering officer of *U564* made the report below, which ended up on Admiral Karl Dönitz's desk. It has been reproduced here from the *Das Archiv*, the journal of the U-boot Archiv.

U564 under Kptlt 'Teddy' Suhren was in the Atlantic, on its fifth operational cruise, when one of the hatches on the upper deck sprang open. A sailor was sent down to fasten it again. The man was holding onto the jumping wire with one hand while using the other to deal with the hatch. This was a little too slow for the commander, who climbed down to give him a hand and promptly fell overboard. The duty watch reacted very quickly and threw him a lifebelt the moment he was alongside the conning tower. The sea was too rough for turning the boat around. Had this been done, it could well have been that the lookouts lost sight of the commander. Therefore the order, 'maximum speed in reverse' was given. Both engines engaged straight away without delay and it was not

U437

The emblem of the elephant also featured on the conning tower shortly the commissioning on 25 October 1941 and it was later also produced as an unofficial cap badge. *U437* was one of the last boats out of a French base on 23 August 1944, when Kptlt Hermann Lamby embarked on a voyage from Bordeaux to Norway, despite the machinery being only partly operational. The remains of the boat were left lying in Bergen when it was totally wrecked during an air raid. Werner-Karl Schultz, the first commander who signed this page, should not be confused with Werner Schulz of *U929*.

WP=13, S=--, K=--

ENQUIRY ABOUT LOSS OF EQUIPMENT

Bootsmann Heinz Webendörfer (UN 1889/35 S) made the following statement:

'On 7 April there occurred some damage to the upper deck which needed to be repaired. The commander came down to help with this and was washed overboard by heavy waves. Once in the water, he discarded the following items: 1 Rain jacket, 1 sou'wester, 1 three-quarter length leather jacket with collar, 1 pair of leather trousers, 1 pair of U-boat boots with cork soles. The commander reported that the jacket and the trousers contained: 1 Mauser pistol of 7.65mm calibre, 1 artillery stop watch, 1 pair of sunglasses with case, 1 artillery torch.

'I wish to appoint Stabsobersteuermann Limburg as witness.'

Stabsobersteuermann Limburg (N 1491 S) made the following statement:

'I was a witness when the commander fell into the water and discarded his clothing together with some items of equipment mentioned in the above statement.'

COMMANDER'S STATEMENT.

'One cannot blame Bootsmann Webendörfer that the commander climbed down onto the upper deck to help repair the damaged hatch cover. Furthermore I do not consider Bootsmann Webendörfer to be responsible for what the commander carries in his pockets. All efforts to retrieve the lost items remained unsuccessful and I should like to request that they be replaced.'

Signed: Suhren.

Above: Kptlt Helmut Rosenbaum of *U2* and *U73*.

Above: Walter Schöppe of *U178*, who took this picture, wrote on the back: 'This is a picture for the family album. The hills of Sumatra can be seen in the background and those who were present know that bananas grow there.'

The men are wearing caps called '*Schiffchen*' (small ship), which were favoured because they folded flat. The swan badge on the right originated during the first voyage under Kpt zur See Hans Ibbeken.

Above: *U443* under Oblt zur See Konstantin von Puttkamer with the 2WO, Gerhard Roch, on the right. One wonders how this picture was taken. Somehow, somebody must have climbed out by supporting themselves on the jumping wires. The fact that the men look so clean and the periscope cover is gleaming would suggest that this was during the first trials shortly after commissioning.

on les aura

Leinen los
es ist soweit
zwo sechs zwo
ist startbereit.

U262

U262 had a remarkable career, participating in a number of dangerous wolfpack attacks under five commanders. She sank four ships, one corvette, but probably her severest test came after in 1944 when she was ordered to sea to challenge the supply routes for the D-Day invasion. Although without a schnorkel, the boat survived to return to the relative safety of her bunker. She travelled through British coastal waters to Flensburgon 5 November 1944, from there sailing to Gotenhafen in the far eastern Baltic to be decommissioned.

WP=11 + 1 short patrol, S=0, K=48

long before the commander was fished back on board.

When he was asked how long he had been in the water, the commander replied that it was at least ten minutes, but a check with a watch indicated that it was no longer than three and a half. During this time, the commander undressed and discarded everything except his underpants. This later led to an inquiry with the flotilla staff to account for the lost pieces (see page 61) and everything except the pistol and the stop watch was replaced by the quartermaster's stores.

The fact that the upper deck could be exceptionally slippery was known by many men, yet often they had no choice other than to negotiate the hazard. The section dealing with submarine escape apparatus mentions that some married and engaged men from *U977* were set ashore in Norway

before Oblt zur See Heinz Schäfer undertook the momentous voyage to South America. Having sealed their private belongings inside water and air-tight escape apparatus and been loaded with some provisions, they were waiting on the upper deck while *U977* approached close to a deserted part of the Norwegian shore. Just as things were looking to be going well, the boat struck a glancing blow against what can best be described as a low sandbank made of granite. These typical features in some fjords are most difficult to spot from a low boat, especially when they are just below the surface of the water. The shock knocked a number of men off their

Above left: Men from *U178* in Bordeaux after their first voyage into the Indian Ocean. A group of Italian submariners donated the crate of oranges.

Above: Men from *U123* with watch officer Ernst Cordes in the centre. Cordes later commanded *U763* and *U1195*, which went down close to Spithead (near Portsmouth in England) exactly one month before the end of the war. The blue woollen caps were naval issue.

feet, throwing them and their possessions into the water, while the rest of the crew struggled to level the boat. A few men close to guns or hand rails managed to hold on, and to launch lifeboats, but things were too hectic and too dangerous for *U977* to return to the shallows to help those in the water. Luckily much of this tiny island was well above the water, making it relatively easy for them clamber out to find shelter among some low scrub. The rest were definitely worse off. The inflatables were blown further out to sea, despite a concerted effort to paddle towards the shore. One wonders what might have happened to them, had it not been for some passing fishermen, who hauled them out of the water in an almost totally exhausted state. At least they were still alive, although Electro Petty Officer Gerhard Kempf, who recorded a statement, lost all his belongings including his camera and a large piece of amber, he had found earlier and carved.

U438

'The Stuka of the Seas ...' was commissioned by Kptlt Rudolf Franzius on 22 November 1941 and, being sponsored by Berlin, carried the coat of arms of the city on the conning tower. Franzius took the boat on three operational patrols into the bitterness of the North Atlantic until March 1943 when he went into hospital and was replaced by Kptlt Heinrich Heinsohn, who went down with the rest of the crew during the subsequent fourth mission, when the boat was depth-charged by the sloop HMS *Pelican*. The word 'Stuka' was derived from *Sturzkampfflugzeug* meaning dive-bomber and was used as a nickname for the classic Junkers Ju87.

WP=4, S=0, K=48

Above left: Lookouts aboard *U382*.

Left: Lookouts aboard *U262*.

Far left: *U163* under Korvkpt Kurt-Eduard Engelmann, with men handling 37mm cartridges.

U-boats Attack

The first six months of war proved quite successfully that the politicians' vision of submarine warfare under Prize Ordinance Regulations only worked in the conference room and was not a great deal of practical use at sea. What was more, this period also showed that the highfalutin' war plans conceived by the Supreme Naval Command did not produce any significant results, other than keeping naval forces occupied by patrolling isolated areas of ocean. Although the occupation of Norway and Denmark in April 1940 was a naval success, the vast majority of U-boats contributed very little, other than demonstrating a major fault with the firing mechanisms of torpedoes. Had it not been for the insistence of a full enquiry from the Commander-in-Chief for U-boats, Konteradmiral Karl Dönitz, these catastrophic failures would probably have been swept under the carpet with a remark from the Torpedo Inspectorate that anyone can make torpedoes fail, if they really try.

Looking back at this period of history it almost appears as if the navy's plans for employing U-boats had failed and therefore, since no one in high authority had any more wise ideas, Dönitz was given a freer hand to run his own show for the summer of 1940. However, he was hampered so seriously by another series of such disastrous torpedo failures that he told Kpt zur See Eberhard Godt, his Chief of Staff, 'We need a few successes. We can't go through this miserable failure a second time.' Utter frustration was still ruling the roost in the Operations Room, when a remarkable commander, born in the Caucasus, Kptlt Viktor Oehrn of *U37*, called in during May 1940 to say he had sunk nine ships in ten days, and two more sinking reports filtered

through during the next three days. The curse of failure was suddenly smashed and the following month saw a steady increase in the number of merchant ships attacked. The figure rose from 18 attacks in May to 74 in June. Attacks have only been counted where the target was sunk or, at least, damaged. Those where nothing was hit have not been included.

June, July and August saw a number of new names appearing in the headlines. Wilhelm Rollmann (*U34*), Fritz Frauenheim (*U21* and *U101*), Engelbert Endrass (*U46*), Heinrich Liebe (*U38*), Hans Jenisch (*U32*), Hans Rösing (*U48*), and many more started to become household names in addition to Günther Prien, Herbert Schultze, Karl Dönitz, Werner Hartmann and Otto Schuhart who already wore Knight's Crosses. These men started rewriting the handbooks by developing their own attacking methods. Instead of shooting a salvo of two or even three torpedoes from a long range of several miles, they approached close enough to hit with one. Following a successful run of seven attacks from 5 to 15 July 1940, Rollmann sent two more merchantmen to the bottom at 14:47 on 26 July and during the following night he fired a torpedo at 02:58, another at 03:05 and a third at 03:13 to sink two ships (the British freighter *Sambre* and motor tanker *Thiera*) from Convoy OB188.

During the next few weeks, the pattern kept repeating itself with other U-boats until the end of August when Erich Topp in *U57* shot all his three bow tubes virtually simultaneously at 00:42 of the 24th to sink the freighters *Saint Dunstan* (5,681 GRT), *Cumberland* (10,939 GRT) and *Havildar* (5,407 GRT). The remarkable point about this achievement was that *U57* had not been designed for the Atlantic. It was a small coastal boat of Type IIC, with only three bow tubes and carrying a total of only five torpedoes. It only reached those far-off

Right: *U121*, **a small coastal boat of Type IIB. The signalman and the absence of lookouts suggest that this photograph was probably taken while entering or leaving port. A wire can be seen running from the radio intake connector to the stout jumping wires which served as aerial and attachment for safety harness when men worked on the upper deck. The other round object, lower down towards the right, is a fog horn.**

waters because French bases provided refuelling facilities close to the vast funnel between Northern Ireland and Scotland, leading into the vastness of the British Western Approaches. Rollmann's boat, *U34*, was a larger Type VIIA, usually carrying 11 torpedoes.

Britain was expecting U-boats to attack while submerged. Instead they approached on the surface during hours of darkness to reap these incredible successes. When Britain realised this, the convoys were faced with the most unfortunate situation where the autumn nights were getting even longer and there was nothing in the armoury to prevent the carnage. Consequently ceremonies for awarding Knight's Crosses became more frequent and the war lurched into what has been called the U-boats' 'Happy Time'.

Allied propaganda has led historians to the general impression that this 'Happy Time' continued until May 1943, when the U-boat offensive suddenly collapsed. However, anyone looking at wartime statistics will see that the successes lasted only until March 1941, when Günther Prien (*U47*), Otto Kretschmer (*U99*), Joachim Schepke (*U100*) and Joachim Matz (*U70*) were sunk in a matter of a few days.

Bearing mind that Otto Kretschmer was the most successful U-boat commander of World War II, Prien was the 9th in tonnage table and Schepke the 11th, then one can see that the next 50 months—or just over four years of war—did not produce the startling successes for the Germans as the first 18 months. Far more U-boats experienced the fatigue of failure rather than the glory of success. It may be interesting to add that *U48*, the most successful U-boat of World War II, left St Nazaire on 22 May 1941 to return to Germany for retirement into the training flotillas. Much of its machinery was so worn out that it was no longer fit to serve in the Atlantic.

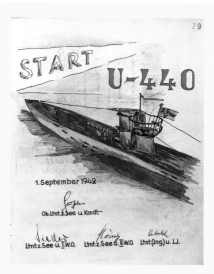

U440

Kptlt Hans Geissler, the first commander of *U440*, remained at the helm for 16 months until April 1943 when he was replaced by Oblt zur See Werner Schwaff. The boat survived Black May 1943 by having been converted into an aircraft trap with additional guns to lure bombers to their deaths, but submarines were too small to mount the type of artillery needed for bringing down large armoured aircraft and all of these special conversions had the additional guns removed again after a brief and dramatically unsuccessful experiment. The boat was sunk on 31 May 1944, a week before the D-Day invasion of Normandy. Geissler survived the war. There was also a U-boat commander with the name of Heinz Geissler, who was killed on 5 July 1944 in Seine Bay when *U390* was sunk.

WP=5, S=0, K=46

Far left: Men of Flotilla Weddigen wearing brand new U-boat leathers. The fact that they are lounging rather keeping lookout would suggest that they are in safe waters, but this picture does give some indication of how cramped the small U-boats were. The flag is flying from the extended attack periscope. It was probably a red one, indicating a U-boat on trials, and was flown especially during diving practice.

Left: A lookout standing by the base of the attack periscope support, aboard *U558* under Kptlt Günther Krech.

The phrase 'glory of success' is, of course, highly inappropriate—the suggestion that any aspect of war could be glorious is sickening in the extreme. In reality, once one removes the glamour from the barbaric actions, one can only see that all wars are cases of one side losing a little less than the other and humanity cannot profit from such. Hans Brunswick, a wartime firefighter in Hamburg said:

'Once you must put all your energy into the basic process of surviving, then you must also discard your emotions or perish. Life is stripped to its barest bones by immense suffering and even those with the remnants of humanity left in them, those who stop to help people in distress, find the only reward can be a painful death. You cannot afford to think. To survive in such barbaric conditions you must act fast and search for your last gram of energy rather than think about feelings.'

The official censor often prevented war correspondents from reporting too deep a level of suffering and the vast majority did not record the cost to human life until it was all over and they could look back at the horrors from the safety of a new age. Indeed, in America much of this suffering was camouflaged by labelling the brave men of the merchant marine as 'draft dodgers' and refusing them veteran status, something that was not given until almost half a century after the war, and then only as a result of the long and tireless protestation from Ian Millar and his group, Sons and Daughters of U.S. Merchant Mariners.

It is rare to read much soul-searching in wartime biographies, but Walter Schöppe's journal about a voyage with *U178*—mentioned in more detail in the chapter On Far Flung Oceans (pp96–105)—is unusual in this respect. Schöppe described two sinkings like this:

'Misty conditions made the morning watch of 10 October 1942 miserable. The lookouts were just in the process of changing when the First Watch Officer, Wilhelm Spahr, spotted a passenger ship dead ahead.

'Action stations. The bow tubes were flooded and the boat lurched onto an attacking course. The approaching ship was zigzagging like mad, but changed course into its own doom by presenting us with a favourable target. Obviously we had not been seen. Yet despite this terrific advantage, all six torpedoes in the tubes had to be shot before one of them produced any results. The first salvo left U178 *at 08:39 hours and it was 11:24 before the* Duchess of Atholl *finally went down.*

'The commander, Kpt zur See Hans Ibbeken, surfaced, but allowed only a few men onto the bridge. The conditions up top were frightening, with women, children and wounded people drifting in lifeboats among a mass of wreckage of wood, crates and God knows what. To make matters even more uncomfortable, everything and everybody seemed to have been covered with a lacing of offensive, black oil. What suffering! What insanity! ...

'... On Friday, 13 November 1942, at 05:30 a steamer was sighted heading directly towards us. Instantly the boat dived for a submerged attack and a short while later the 3,764GRT freighter Louise

U460

U460 was the second specially built supply submarine of Type XIV, whence this rather appropriate sketch. Although launched at Deutsche Werke in Kiel on the same day as the first supply boat (U459), finishing off took a little longer and it was Christmas Eve of 1941 before U460 was commissioned by Kptlt Friedrich Schäfer, who later took the boat on two patrols. Kptlt Ebe Schnoor then commanded U460 for a further five patrols, although one of these was only two days long. The machinery failed the deep diving test and therefore he returned to Bordeaux for repairs.

WP=6, S=0, K=62

Opposite page, above: *U128*, a long-range boat of Type IXC/40.

Opposite page, below: *U69*, a Type VIIC under Kptlt Jost Metzler, showing the early conning tower layout. The support of the attack periscope, with a sighting compass attached, is nearest the gun platform. The torpedo aimer is situated behind the two men on the right and the top of the navigation periscope can be seen on the right. The slot in the conning tower wall houses the circular radio direction finder. The two flagpoles were usually removed before diving. The single 20mm anti-aircraft gun suggests that this was taken early in the war, but after the inverted wind deflectors, at the top of the conning tower, were introduced.

Left: A different type of torpedo aimer; these sights were rotated by twisting the collar, which the man is gripping.

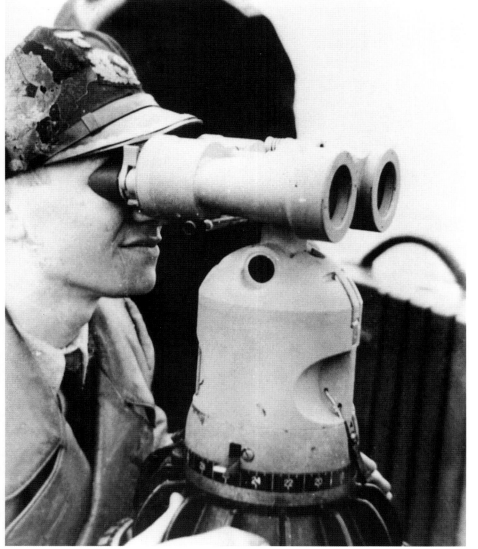

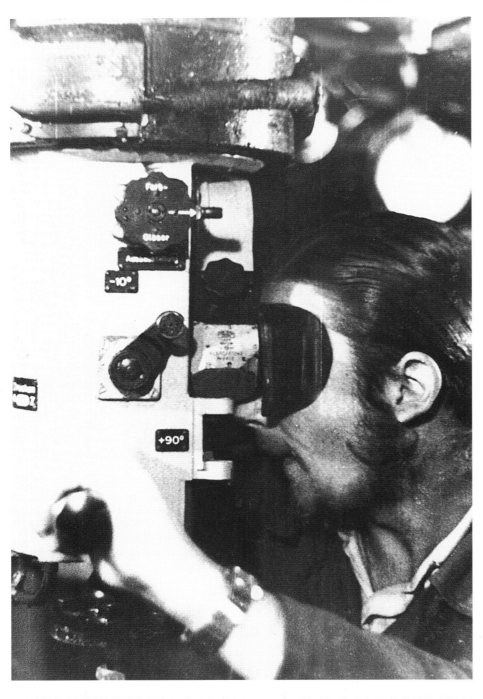

Left: Most U-boats had two periscopes: one with a small head for attacking and another with a larger lens for navigation and for observing the sky. In large boats of Types IX both these terminated inside the conning tower, but on Types VII and smaller, only the attack periscope could be operated from the commander's attacking position inside the conning tower and the other periscope was viewed from the central control room, one deck down. Since space was so tight in the conning tower, the majority of these 'commander at the periscope' type of pictures were taken down below in the central control room. The attack periscope in the majority of boats was fitted with a saddle so that the whole affair could be rotated by pressing on a button with either the left or right foot.

Moller *disappeared below the waves. Later, after surfacing, Wilhelm Spahr was somewhat subdued at seeing a man on a liferaft wave at the U-boat. Seeing no action was being taken, he informed the commander that the man by their side was in need of medical assistance, but Hans Ibbeken refused to help. He told the men on the bridge to think about how their own people at home were suffering, but even allowing the horror of bombing roam through one's mind didn't drive away the madness of the times were are living in. What barbarity we have to endure.'*

Of all the torpedoes carried into the Atlantic, only a very tiny fraction of the total actually hit a target. A much greater proportion was brought home again or missed. Using the information in Peter Sharpe's book *U-boat Factfile*, a rough estimate suggests that over 36,000 torpedoes were carried to sea. The maximum number of ships sunk was about 2,775, so there was a substantial discrepancy between the actual and potential successes.

Since the history of the war is more often concerned with success, and tends to mention suffering and failures only if they were highly dramatic, it might be of interest to look at some of those occasions which ended with a depressed curse. Once again we can look into Walter Schöppe's journal:

'U178 *marked its entry into the Indian Ocean by turning north. The weather was most unusual, with the seas coming from that direction and the wind from the south-west. It appeared as if the water didn't know what it was supposed to be doing, since currents were running into each other from all unexpected angles. Trial dives and depth-keeping exercises dominated much of the day and nerves were highly strung* when the radio room intercepted a message from *U198* under *Korvkpt Werner Hartmann*. "British freighter *Northmoor, 4,392 GRT*, sunk on 17 May 1943 at 28°27'S 32°43E.'

'Korvkpt Wilhelm Dommes, the new commander of *U178*, assumed that this was part of a convoy out of Durban (South Africa) and ordered an increase in speed, hoping to get further news from Hartmann or Korvkpt Eitel-Friedrich Kentrat in *U196*, who was also nearer the scene of action.

'Contradictory news during the course of the following day made finding the convoy even more difficult and totally impossible to guess where the ships might be. To make matters even worse, shortly before 21:00 hours a continuous tone from the radar detector drove us into the cellar and nothing at all was picked up by the underwater sound detector, suggesting that the radar transmitter had been aboard an aircraft.

'When we surfaced cautiously, the volume of the receiver increased so enormously that the piercing tone could be heard without earphones. There followed another alarm dive. Again there were no sounds and we surfaced again. This time, two illuminated aircraft were spotted, apparently working together and Dommes turned south, away from them, but keeping these persistent nuisances in sight. The radar signals became rather faint, indicating that we were moving further away from the source. Then, suddenly, without warning, the radar detector burst out at full volume, suggesting something was very close-by. At the same time lookouts reported that the aircraft had switched their lights off and, once more, we dropped into an alarm dive. Dommes sat in his small corner, obviously thinking through his options and quickly decided to run away at fast speed to bring us closer to the coast and hopefully ahead of the convoy.

'It was an hour and five minutes past midnight of 19 May 1943 when we surfaced again. The radar detector indicated that there was considerable activity in our area and it could well be that the aircraft were patrolling the space above the convoy. Yet, all searching proved to be useless. It was impossible to find Hartmann's convoy and in the end Dommes gave up and allowed frustration to rule the roost. To make matters even more infuriating, a number of sighting reports came flooding in, but all them too far away to be of any use for us.

'24 May 1943 was just two hours old when the detector indicated the presence of a radar set in the vicinity. Dommes dived instantly with the idea of remaining undetected. Three hours later we surfaced again, but were none the wiser with regard to the opposition's position. This time, at 05:05 hours, a faint column of smoke came into sight. Although it was still dark, a bright moon provided enough light to

identify two ships and a number of smaller vessels, probably escorts, but these were such a good distance ahead of the merchant ships that they had already passed us, so we were in a good position to attack. At this crucial moment, while Dommes was deciding on the best approach, the convoy obliged by turning towards us. The target was excellent, although a few sharp manoeuvres at periscope depth allowed the bows and stern to break through the surface of the water. The sound detector suggested that we had not been seen, everything was perfect, except that it was now impossible to open the stern tubes and the confusion lasted long enough for the target to move out of range. The massive boat was too cumbersome to turn for shooting with the bow tubes

'Despite the absence of targets, there was no shortage of aircraft in these far-flung reaches of the British Empire. They were becoming a real nuisance. It was around 02:00 hours of 28 May 1943 when the radar detector indicated activity in our vicinity. Once again Dommes ordered "action stations". This time he was more successful. Remaining submerged for two hours, the noises gradually increased in volume until it was time to surface again. The lookouts were hardly on the bridge, when *U178* vanished once more into depths. "It's a hospital ship," announced Dommes. "We can't attack that."

'Lying very close to Cape St Francis, we remained lurking for three days, waiting for a convoy, but nothing was seen other than a small fishing boat and the aircraft pests, which were making life so difficult that it was necessary to remain submerged for most of the time.

'Then, the final blow to our self-esteem came at a time when the batteries were exhausted, forcing *U178* to the surface. At that vulnerable time, when another prolonged dive was impossible, a convoy of

U463

Korvkpt Leo Wolfbauer, was one of the very few commanders who also served in submarines during World War I. Born in 1895, he became watch officer in *U29* just before the end of the hostilities in 1918. On his first mission with *U463*, he supplied 12 submarines in mid-Atlantic; on his second 13; on his third 15; and on his fourth 20. His boat was sunk with all 56 men on board by a Halifax of No 58 Squadron, RAF, piloted by Flg Off A. J. W. Birch, on 16 May 1943, making it one of the statistics which contributed towards the disastrous losses of Black May.

WP=5, S=0, K=56

Far left: Before the war, Germany developed a magnetic torpedo detonator to explode underneath the target. These turned out to be unreliable and many U-boats had to work with contact detonators and these did not guarantee a sinking. This shows the 1,974 GRT Norwegian freighter *Tolosa* being sunk by *U108* under Klaus Scholtz. The ship left Kingston, Jamaica on 1 February 1942 for Chester, PA (USA) but was sunk a week later.

Left: The *Obersteuermann* or navigator at his chart table aboard *U18*. There were times when the sun and stars were obscured for days, making it impossible to determine an accurate position, but there were also occasions when the course had to be calculated with a stop watch—such as when someone fell overboard.

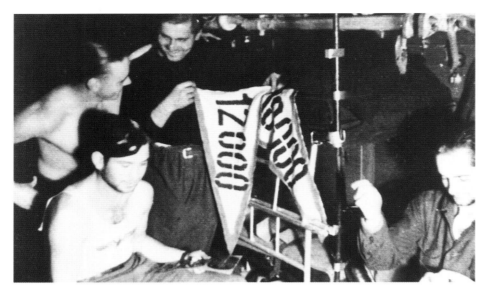

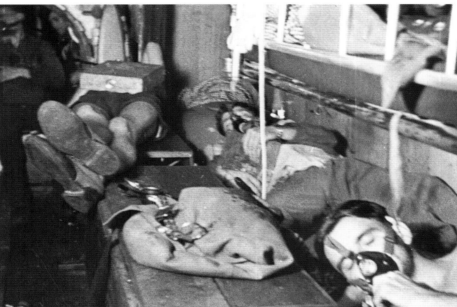

6–10 ships appeared. There was nothing Dommes could do, other than instruct the radio room to send a sighting report. The level of frustration inside the boat was exceedingly high, but there was nothing which could be done about it. The threat from aircraft was too strong to consider any foolhardy action and all Dommes could do was to withdraw. To make matters even worse, a number of success reports from other boats were intercepted. It was as if we have been bewitched.'

The following are some extracts from the log of the Portuguese sloop *Alfonso de Albuquerque* which left Laurenco Marques (Mozambique, Africa) with the specific purpose of picking up survivors from the British troopship *Nora Scotia*. The 6,796 GRT *Nova Scotia* called on Massawa (Ethiopia, East Africa) and then headed south without escort, but with about 1,200 people squashed on board, to be torpedoed by *U177* under Korvkpt Robert Gysae during the first breakfast sitting of 28 November 1942. This mass of suffering humanity was made up of a mixture of nationalities including some 766 Italian civilian internees, several hundred Africans and a good number of British soldiers, some

Top: U-boats usually hoisted 'success' pennants to indicate the number and size of of ships they had attacked. Since this was a 'ship-made' fad, there were no hard and fast rules about the flag's appearance. This photograph was taken in *U124*, a highly successful Type IXB, which was commissioned by Georg-Wilhelm Schulz and later commanded by Johann—but better known as Jochen—Mohr.

Above: It seems highly likely that this is *U31*, a Type VIIA, commanded first by Rolf Dau, then by Johannes Habekost and later by Wilfried Prellberg. The men are wearing breathing apparatus which extracted carbon dioxide from their exhaled breath. The man on the right is lying on a table, half of which has been folded down so that it does not obstruct the whole passageway. In the back is a circular doorway through a pressure resistant bulkhead leading to the central control room.

Right: Wars can only be fought as long as there is a powerful propaganda system to whip a fighting spirit into youngsters, and with such powerfully emotional support, it is no wonder that soldiers enjoyed their success. Even today the media still perpetuates the image of bravery and glory, and does not project strongly enough the suffering inflicted by war. This photograph show survivors from the 2,669 GRT Norwegian freighter *Breiviken*, sunk by *U178* under Korvkpt Wilhelm Dommes on 4 July 1943. Whatever their nationality or religion or whatever they might have believed in, they were all human beings doing difficult job in unnatural surroundings and had had to endure the immense pain of being shipwrecked. For a long time I thought that Charles Walker of Manchester was unique in having had three ships sunk beneath him, yet he is by no means alone.

of whom were employed as guards while others were on their way home for leave.

'28 November 1942 at 22:45 hours, saw a British warship and gave them the position of the sinking, but the ship wasn't interested and continued on its way.

'29 November, following a chain of continuous rescues with the ship's cutters helping exhausted people in the water, the sun went down on an empty sea.

'20:15 hours, picked up one man floating in the water.

'21:05 hours, saw a red Very light and then switched on our searchlight to find a raft with four men and another person clinging to a piece of wood.

'21:40 hours, picked up one man swimming in the water.

'We came across several boats and rafts with squabbling people.

'05:45, we are steaming through hundreds of dead bodies floating in the water. It all looks very calm and no one on board appears to be disturbed by the horrific sight. The earlier experience, when we came across men fighting for space on liferafts was far more troublesome, especially for our cadets. The hate among the survivors was so strong that they would

not allow other nationalities aboard their raft. Only once did we find a raft with people speaking different languages.

'05:55, rescued three men from a water-filled lifeboat. The weather is getting worse. Had this rough sea set in earlier, it would have been impossible to rescue the hundreds of people we picked up.

'16:15, set course for Laurenco Marques. There is no hope of finding more survivors. The ship's doctor, two male nurses and a number of volunteers have worked for 36 hours, saving the lives of several people ... It was necessary to separate the various nationalities because fights were breaking out ... We were surprised by the endurance of the survivors, including the women. Some of them had been swimming in the water for over 36 hours ... One women jumped from a raft to reach us, but vanished below the waves and never reappeared ... A number of our cadets were disappointed that a British officer died from a heart attack shortly after they had resuscitated him with artificial respiration ... Sadly the sharks killed almost a quarter of the survivors ... Despite our careful search, some men were missed, but one turned up ten days later on the East African coast.'

U508

'This is how we are going to grip them ...' and they did! Kptlt Georg Staats took the boat on seven operational voyages, sinking 14 ships in a relatively short period of time between 15 October 1942 and 11 May 1943. This is quite surprising since the boat came home empty-handed from the first patrol to the Caribbean and the Gulf of Mexico. Being in port for much of the Black May in 1943 didn't help the men of *U508*. Leaving Lorient again on 3 July, all 54 on board this Type IXC were killed when they came under attack in the Bay of Biscay from a Liberator of No 224 Squadron, RAF. The aircraft, piloted by Lt R. B. Brownell of the United States Navy, crashed as a result of gunfire from the U-boat, killing everybody on board. So this was one of those cases where both sides killed each other.

WP=7, S=0, K=54

Above: Lucky survivors? As extracts from the log of the Portuguese sloop *Alfonso de Albuquerque* shows, getting into the lifeboats didn't always guarantee survival. This is a lifeboat photographed from *U178*.

On Patrol with *U48*

The most successful boat of the war laid mines off Weymouth on England's south coast and went on to become the first to pass the psychological barrier of sinking 100.000 tons of shipping.

Kptlt Herbert Schultze had just passed the Orkneys during his homeward-bound voyage in December 1939. when the radio operator handed him a signal. It wasn't good news. The U-boat Command ordered a drastic change in course to avoid a new protective minefield laid in the German Bight. Schultze cursed. something he didn't do very often. He hadn't anticipated the extra distance and had already consumed the engineering officer's 'private' fuel reserve during the intensity of the hunt. Now Kptlt (Ing) Willi Lohner's face suggested they might not make it all the way back to Kiel. This would normally not have mattered, but the delay in being refuelled could prevent some of the men from getting home for Christmas. Funkobergefreiter Walter Lang, for example, was faced with a long journey to Karlsruhe, deep in Germany's south, making it vital for him to reach the railway station before the public transport system slowed down for the festivities.

Some of the men could have left the boat by the massive locks in Brunsbüttel. There was a branch line to Itzehoe with good connections to Hamburg and *U48* had enough north Germans on board to take the boat the last few miles to Kiel, but the men hadn't washed nor shaved for several weeks and sending them off in such a filthy state would create more problems than it solved. even if the U-boat Command should agree to such unorthodox action. After all. they had an image to maintain. *U48* had featured in cinema newsreels and the high standards expected by the general public could not be compromised by an offensive smell of unwashed body odour. Despite coming over as soft as a brush, 'Daddi' Schultze maintained the highest of standards with the strictest of discipline, even if it involved missing Christmas at home.

In the end, *U48* reached Kiel with both diesels still running and there was enough time for clearing out the interior before the men got their well-earned rest. Schultze's wish to get them home for Christmas

wasn't solely a case of the commander's benevolence, but a persistent two-edged sword of wanting his men back refreshed for the next operation. The notion that this could well be their last Christmas, didn't feature often in his thinking and, when it did, he forced it right into the back of his mind. Such cold reality could not be mulled over too frequently, otherwise the mind would have prevented the body from making that extra sacrifice demanded by the war.

By the time hawsers were being made fast. the moist and moderate south-westerly, which had accompanied *U48* back from the Scilly Islands, had turned into a bitterly cold easterly. Although this assured a white Christmas and a slippery new year, it also converted the waters in Kiel harbour into a white, solid desert. By the end of January it was no longer safe for a submarine to be out alone anywhere near the harbour and *U48* cautiously made her way across the water to have an ice cap

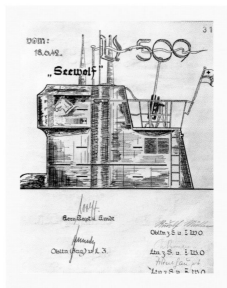

U509

U509 was called 'Seawolf' after the commander, Korvkpt Karl-Heinz Wolff, who took *U509* on only one patrol to the Caribbean before being shunted into the destroyer *Z15* as first watch officer. From there he was pushed into a number of land-based positions, suggesting there were some problems with his first command. The Berliner, Kptlt Werner Witte, went down with *U509* on 15 July 1943 while on his third patrol with this boat. During this period of time, he succeeded in sinking six ships and damaging three more. However this spell of good luck did not last and all 54 men on board were killed when it was attacked with Fido homing-torpedoes by an aircraft from the carrier USS *Santee*.

WP=4, S=0, K=54

fitted at the Deutsche Werke ship yard. Theoretically this should have provided the necessary protection to negotiate the Kiel Canal, but even the icebreaker, the old battleship *Hessen*, which had been converted to become a remote-controlled artillery target, was having incredible difficulties clearing a path for the small submarine. The men in *U48* took it all in good heart and didn't ask who had given the senseless order to depart under such chronic conditions. Schultze stood on the bridge, together with the almost superfluous canal pilot, both of them wrapped in thick leathers and wearing as much as they could. 'Vaddi' (Daddi), as the men called him, was easily recognisable by an oversized muff and fur hat, which made him look slightly pregnant. But nobody bothered what you looked like. The important point was to be as comfortable as the hostile elements allowed.

The men had the consolation that conditions were bound to improve once

Above left: World War II was two days old when this photograph was taken from *U48* under Kptlt Herbert or 'Vaddi' (Daddy) Schultze. It shows a lifeboat from the 4,852 GRT British freighter *Royal Sceptre*. During those early days of the war, there were still opportunities for a more humane approach to the sinking of ships. A short while later, *U48* stopped another ship and ordered it to change course to pick up these survivors.

they reached the turbulent salt of the North Sea. Yet, this time, that general rule of thumb didn't apply. The vastness of the Elbe estuary looked like a rockery without any sight of the fierce tidal currents. Normally the entire area would have been shut down for all traffic, but it was war and the tiny U-boat had to go on—but not without an ice escort and this, too, was having its own problems. Somewhere among that mass of unwelcoming hard slabs was the tug *Löwe*, struggling with orders to accompany a U-boat into open water. The low temperatures didn't allow *U48* to keep to the Naval Command's schedule through the thick ice, leaving *U48* no alternative but to make fast on the canal side of the locks and wait. Having worked for half a day in the excruciating cold, Schultze allowed the men ashore for the afternoon. A few warmed up by helping elderly locals shovel snow and were rewarded with an ample supply of grog around warm tile ovens.

The following day, progress was exactly as the men had predicted. The pressure of the ice floes prevented the engines from being run up to any significant speed, leaving no alternative but for the powerful and more versatile tug to tow *U48* into raging currents of the Elbe, but even when they got there, they didn't find any open water. The entire river was such a solid mass that anyone capable of keeping their feet on slippery surfaces could have walked from one side to the other. That would have been no mean feat since the river is almost three kilometres wide at this point.

Conditions weren't much better by the lightship *Elbe II*, but at least there was sufficient water between the floes for *U48* to continue under her own power. However, Schultze was not heading out to sea. The heavy bow protection cap for the ice had to be removed and the propellers sounded like an out-of-tune steel band, giving him no alternative other than to make for Heligoland harbour. There *U48* made fast next to Kptlt Gustav-Adolf Mugler (*U41*), who was used to such foul conditions. Having been brought up in Danzig meant that he was accustomed to the sea freezing over for part of the year. Schultze wasn't going to risk the lives of his men by sending them down with emergency diving gear while ice floes were adding to the hazards. Someone with the appropriate qualifications and proper equipment could do the dodgy work. Having reported the details of damage to the Commander-in-Chief for U-boats, the men made use of the facilities before obeying their orders to make for Wilhelmshaven, the nearest port with adequate repair facilities.

Four days later *U48* was back in Heligoland with new propellers. The bow

shield was removed and then *U48* headed out for her fourth operational war cruise. The ice problem diminished and no one could find any reasons for a few more unplanned hours in port. Steaming north, the men settled into their usual, monotonous routine of avoiding the opposition. Willi Lohner had been replaced by a new engineering officer, Lt zur See (Ing) Erich Zürn, who desperately needed time to work himself in and have an opportunity to 'play' with the U-boat. Schultze handed over control to him, allowing him to run through a number of manoeuvres and to get the feel of a real operational piece of steel. The 33-year old from Stuttgart, with experience aboard the ill-fated heavy cruiser *Admiral Hipper*, brought with him the powerful charisma, which drove him on to become the second engineering officer to be awarded the Knight's Cross. It was Gerd Suhren, the brother of *U48*'s first watch officer—Reinhard or 'Teddy' Suhren—who became the first engineer to receive the Knight's Cross. This was awarded in October 1940, just six months before Zürn's.

Zürn's introduction to an operational Type VIIB U-boat was not terribly happy. Things didn't quite work out as he had anticipated. Never before had Zürn experienced serious problems trimming a submarine, but somehow, someone in *U48* was testing his abilities to the limit. And that person could only be the commander. Although relatively young, at the age of 30 Schultze was already known as 'Daddy' and his reputation didn't fit into the callous image which was forming in Zürn's mind. Schultze was not the type to make special problems for his men. So what was the trouble? Why the bloody hell couldn't Zürn get his act together? Why was this hulk of steel behaving so differently from the training boats? The realisation that Schultze was also having problems with the boat's behaviour peculiarities calmed Zürn's mind and dismissed the idea that he was being put to the test by an overzealous commander. That blasted mass of steel really did have a mind of its own and obviously didn't want do what was demanded of it.

Having established that it was not the inability of the engineering officer nor a spanner thrown in by the commander which was to blame, both men started searching for the culprit. The first obvious move was to blame the steel protection cap, but all the bits had been removed and could not be the cause for making the boat bow heavy. A little time was required before the *Groschen* (a German penny) dropped. Following the second operational tour the streamlined fairings in front of the four bow torpedo tubes had been removed and *U48* sailed without them for the third voyage. New ones had been fitted during

U522

Kptlt Herbert Schneider says on this page that the 5th U-Flotilla is '*Der besten organisierten Flotilla*'— the best organised flotilla. One wonders whether he was biased or being diplomatic, since the flotilla commander, Karl-Heinz Moehle, commanded *U123* while Schneider was first watch officer. Whatever, he took *U522* on two war patrols, attacking and at least damaging nine ships. Consequently he was awarded the Knight's Cross on 16 January 1943 after having left Lorient for his second patrol on New Year's Eve. Unfortunately he did not live long enough to receive the highly coveted award. *U522* was sunk with all 51 on board on 23 February 1943 when depth-charged by the sloop HMS *Totland* under Lt-Cdr L. E. Woodhouse.

WP=2, S=0, K=51

Opposite: The sinking of the 7,176 GRT American Liberty Ship *Alice F. Palmer* on 10 July 1943 after a prolonged chase. Two torpedoes were required to slow her down and then almost 100 shells were fired from the large, 105mm deck gun before the action was over. After that, it still took a while before the burning wreck finally slipped below the waves.

the recent spell in port, but it looked as if the additional ballast, to compensate for their absence, had not been removed, and these four doors of steel added up to a ton in weight. Schultze could only kick himself. His old engineering officer would have noticed at once, but Zürn didn't have enough experience with Type VIIB submarines to recognise the additional difficulty—instead he put the peculiarity of trim down to his own stupidity.

Schultze was not the sort of bloke to look around for scapegoats and quickly agreed with Zürn that they could make their way to Weymouth harbour at top speed and thereby empty the fuel in the bunkers nearest the bows, to reduce the weight. The problem of the bows dipping deep into the waves also threw the mining operation into a totally different perspective. At first the men in *U48* had been hoping they might get out of the imposition of crawling up on a British harbour by finding more lucrative targets elsewhere and perhaps being ordered home before the eggs could be deposited. Now, suddenly, the mines gave the men an opportunity of making the boat glide better through the waves.

Putting out to sea with additional ballast was not *U48*'s only mistake. On the seventh day at sea, Schultze committed one of those unforgivable blunders, for which he kicked himself. It was just after midday on 7 January 1940 when lookouts reported a large streamer coming towards them. Alarm bells drove the boat below the waves while the sound detector confirmed the target was maintaining its course right towards the lurking U-boat. A quick glance through the periscope enabled Schultze to estimate a size of about 7,000–8,000GRT. As additional bait, he made out a large gun on the stern and a significant rangefinder above the bridge. It had to be an auxiliary cruiser! What else would carry such a large rangefinder? The men had already been at action stations for half and hour or so when Tube 2 was fired at a range of 700m. It was a classic attack. The order 'fire' was given just as the ship was sideways-on. The 'eel' had to hit. There was no way it could miss. Everything was perfect, except that it was too late by the time Schultze realised that he had dialled 332° instead of 322° in the target speed compensator. Consequently he could only kick himself and hope that his men would excuse the oversight.

A light wind was blowing up from the southwest when *U48* lay in 36m of water on the seabed off Start Point, by Devon's southernmost tip. Men of the duty watch, who had to move about, wrapped their shoes in rags, to prevent unnecessary noise giving away their presence. Later, when it was dark again, *U48* surfaced into the unknown and, what was far more critical,

into an exceptionally black night. Lighthouse illumination seemed to have been switched off and there was no way anyone could get an accurate fix on anything. Readings taken the previous day gave the men a pretty good idea where they were, but now they found the night so dark that lookouts could dispense with binoculars. It was impossible to see the bows or stern as the engines pushed *U48* eastwards, towards the Shambles lightship, or at least to the position where the men thought it should be. Running quietly so that lookouts could hear approaching ships, the men hoped to avoid a collision. An encroaching white mist rolling through the blackness made the whole effort feel like some exaggerated scene from a horror movie rather than a serious attempt of laying mines in the approaches of Weymouth harbour. What was more, navigation had to be perfect because the Royal Navy had laid a defensive mine barrage shortly after the earlier call by *U26*, to prevent intrusion from gate-crashers. However, the British Admiralty had also used a somewhat dated cipher system to announce the fact and the German Radio Monitoring Service succeeded in identifying the gaps for legitimate ships passing in and out. It was these gaps which *U48* was hoping to plug with a few surprises.

Despite the difficulties of navigating through nil visibility, Schultze maintained his principle of steering only courses divisible by the lucky number seven. The helmsman automatically checked every course ordered by the bridge and if it wasn't divisible by seven, he would choose the nearest number that was! Wondering where they were and hoping that their calculations with the depth indicator were correct, Schultze was surprised by a destroyer, which didn't take any notice of the U-boat. Following this a few lights were sighted, giving the impression that the old, prewar navigation lights were still functioning, albeit with reduced visibility. The men in *U48* had the feeling of being in the right position, but they could not make a positive sighting to confirm the hunch. This gave Schultze the agonising choice of either dropping the mines or heading out to sea for a second attempt during the following night. At that critical moment came a stroke of luck. *U48* almost collided with the Shambles lightship! The jubilation quickly dissolved when Schultze realised that the ship could have been moved into a different position. But then, on second thoughts, he considered this to have been unlikely. Such a move would also confuse the opposition's commercial traffic. Schultze didn't fancy the prospects of sitting around for another day, so close to solid parts of England and nobody was showing any enthusiasm for repeating the

U581

U581 left Kiel on 13 December 1941 under Kptlt Werner Pfeifer. The date was perhaps an unlucky number, but the day before was even more unlucky. The 12th was a Friday and there was a strong tradition in the German Navy never to leave a home port on a Friday, so sailing was postponed until the early hours of the 13th. Having called at St Nazaire, ostensibly for refuelling, the men spent Christmas with the 7th Flotilla before heading out into the Atlantic, where the boat was sunk by the escort HMS *Westcott* on 2 February 1942. Everybody found an orderly way out of sinking boat and the majority of men were picked up by the destroyer, whose commander (Cdr I. H. Brockett-Hugh) even apologised for one his men having fired a depth charge after the cease-fire without orders. The second watch officer, Lt zur See Walter Sitek, avoided becoming a prisoner of war by swimming for five hours towards the island of Pico, from where he was taken to Spain aboard a Portuguese destroyer and eventually he made his way back to Germany. Later he became commander of *U17*, *U981* and *U3005*.

WP=2, S=41, K=4

Left: An ocean-going boat with wide upper deck struggling through coastal ice, experiencing similar conditions to those endured by *U48* when setting out for its fourth war voyage.

nerve-tingling venture. So, there and then Schultze made the decision. Now or never! By 04:00 hours everybody in *U48* was pleased that the water under the keel was getting deeper and that they were heading out to sea, back towards the southwestern tip of Ireland. Although noticeably warmer than in Germany, the persistent wind was moist and often powerful enough to drench the duty watch on top of the conning tower, making it cold, wet and highly unpleasant to patrol those waters.

Earlier, when the men were returning from leave, they found the torpedo mines rather disappointing. Everybody knew that *U48* was in the running for becoming the first U-boat to reach that critical target of sinking 100,000GRT of shipping. There was no certainty of reaching that goal with mines and gave other contenders in the unofficial race an excellent opportunity of overtaking. Günther Prien of *U47*, Joachim Schepke of *U100* and several others were well on the way to beating *U48* past the post. What's more, Otto Kretschmer's combined tonnage with *U23* and *U99* was also getting close and he could steal the limelight. After all, although he had been in two boats, most of the crew changed with him, so really it was still the same body of men.

It is a reflection on Schultze's integrity when one realises that he was awarded the Knight's Cross shortly after having reported sinking a total of 16 ships with 112,757GRT and postwar calculations showed this to have been 16 ships of 109,074GRT. A discrepancy of only 3,683GRT. Many commanders wildly overestimated their successes and the U-boat Command generally overcalculated by an average of at least a third. So, Schultze's modest reckoning was incredibly accurate for those hectic war conditions.

Herbert Schultze became the third officer in the Kriegsmarine and the second U-boat commander to be awarded the Knight's Cross. The first one had gone to Günther Prien for sinking the battleship HMS *Royal Oak* in the Royal Navy's anchorage at Scapa Flow.

Having cleared the bow torpedo compartment of mines, *U48* settled much better into the water and was free to exploit the eight torpedoes to their fullest. However, the men were not in luck. The first ships to pass were illuminated neutrals and it wasn't until three days later that a suspicious looking character approached by steering a zigzag course. What followed was not the easiest of decisions for Schultze. Surfacing close to the quarry, the duty watch poured out of the conning tower hatch while the 1WO, 'Teddy' Suhren, challenged the Dutch freighter with a signal lamp, ordering the master to bring his ship's papers to the submarine. Schultze then recorded the following reasons for sinking the ship:

'The *Burgerdyk* made me suspicious by steering a zigzag course.

'The master told me that he was running into an English control port to have his cargo examined.

'Our radio room has a very strong suspicion that the ship transmitted a U-boat sighting report shortly before we attacked.

'Part of the cargo listed in ship's papers is definitely classified as war contraband.'

Schultze ordered the *Burgerdyk* to send a distress call, saying that she had been in a collision and was sinking. This was repeated by the Land's End Coastguard, while the Dutch steamer *Edam* confirmed that she was 110 nautical miles to the south and coming up fast to help. Schultze gave the First Watch Officer, 'Teddy' Suhren, permission to shoot one torpedo and then made off to put some distance between himself and the by now well-advertised sinking.

One of the awkward problems was that the Type VII carried two and the Type IX four torpedoes in external storage containers from which they could not be fired. The idea of accommodating all the torpedoes in discharge tubes was not considered until much later in the war and such a boat was never built. Therefore, it was often necessary to find a suitable opportunity to transfer these heavy, one-and-a-half ton objects from the outside of the boat. On this occasion the men fitted a special canvas screen, invented and designed by Schultze himself, to keep the force of the waves off the men working on the exposed upper deck. Surprisingly it worked rather well, keeping the interior of the boat much dryer than before. Yet, despite this, Schultze still cursed, complaining that the tackle for moving torpedoes was far too heavy and clumsy for use in such precarious conditions. After all, they were also working in total darkness. Despite the problems, both torpedoes were safely brought below. It is worth reflecting that the men were in the Atlantic, off southern Ireland during February—not an ideal time to be carrying out such hard physical work on the low deck, where cold waves constantly threatened to wash the drenched bodies into the raging sea. In addition to this, there was the constant danger of water gushing into the interior through open torpedo hatches.

The big stroke of luck came six hours later, at 04:00 hours on 12 February 1940, when a convoy was sighted heading straight towards *U48*. The duty watch on the top of the conning tower had finished counting 15 ships with four escorts and what looked like an aircraft carrier, when the nearest escort came haring towards them. Diving right in front of the merchant

U584

Kptlt Joachim Deecke, whose older brother commanded *U1* and perished in the North Sea on 6 April 1940, landed four agents at Jacksonville in Florida in June 1942. The boat was on its eleventh operational patrol on 31 October 1940 when it was sunk with all 53 hands, including a number of men from the radio monitoring service, who were on board to check on Allied high frequency radio waves. Jürgen Deecke was born on 28 April 1911 in the Free and Hansa Town of Lübeck on the Baltic coast, famous for its good quality marzipan.

WP=10 + 1 transit patrol, S=0, K=53

Above left: *U48* with the IIWO, Lt zur See Otto Ites, on the left and Bootsmaat Otto Petzokat during the boat's third war voyage. Otto Ites later became a commander, was awarded the Knight's Cross and survived when *U94* was sunk on 27 August 1942. His twin brother, Rudolf, was not so lucky. He was killed as commander of *U709* on 1 March 1944.

Left: Men relaxing on the deck of *U48* during the fourth war voyage, which included a mining operation off Weymouth on England's south coast. The man on the left is wearing a captured British helmet.

U591

This dramatic picture with stirring words marks the beginning of a comparatively successful period during difficult times when five ships were sunk and one more was damaged. Kptlt Hans-Jürgen Zetsche served as first watch officer in *U28* and *U10* before commanding *U20*, *U8*, *U4*, *U560*, *U378* and, finally, *U591*. He cheated death during Black May 1943 by ending up in hospital in St Nazaire. Being there for a period of nine months would suggest that this was no superficial injury. The second commander, Oblt zur See Reimar Ziesmer, also commanded several boats such as *U145* and *U236* and he was also lucky to cheat death when *U591* was sunk by being made a prisoner of war near Recife in Brazil, together with 27 other men. The boat was attacked by a Ventura aircraft of VP-107 Squadron, USN, which caused it to go down exceedingly quickly. The survivors were later picked up by USS *Saucy*.

WP=9, S=28, K=19

Left: The last remnants of the 7,129 GRT Canadian steamer *Jasper Park*, which was sunk on 6 July 1943.

ships, *U48* could only hope that the commotion of so much noise would prevent the warships from coming close enough for a depth-charge attack. Schultze was not the sort to be put off for long. Grabbing the opportunity, he made a last desperate attempt to shoot at least one torpedo. This plan had just formulated in his mind, when he realised that they had not properly compensated for the different positions of two torpedoes. Consequently the boat dropped uncontrollably down to 80m. Zürn battled to bring the boat slowly higher, but without breaking the surface. This was, indeed, a painful experience and an agonising wait, but the new engineering officer's ability didn't let *U48* down. The snag was that when Schultze peered through the periscope he found the interior so steamed up that he couldn't see. This vicious gremlin was due to human error, and this time it wasn't Schultze's fault. One of the new men had taken it upon himself to follow standing orders, learned in *U45*, to switch on the periscope heater. Unknown to him, this had been prohibited by Schultze because of the dramatic condensation problem. However, none of the men in *U48* was a total beginner and the boat was still brought close enough for a submerged attack against a large, blurred shadow. This time the angle deflector was

adjusted for the wrong setting and Schultze missed again.

Surfacing a short while later, *U48* reported the find and almost immediately received instructions from the U-boat Command to keep the ships in sight. *U37* (Werner Hartmann), *U26* (Heinz Scheringer), *U28* (Günter Kuhnke) and *U29* (Otto Schuhart) were all within range. At that moment it looked as if this was going to be the day of the wolfpack! For the first time in five months, there was a mass of boats in the same area. The vision of the wolfpack could become reality. It been practised during prewar manoeuvres, Dönitz had been trying hard to get such a group to sea, but so far with incredibly limited success, and now *U48* seemed to be on the verge of making the breakthrough. The first large scale wolfpack attack! However, Schultze didn't count his chickens too early, despite escorts taking no further interest in him. It was now 08:00 hours and a whole day's worth of steaming would be required before it was dark enough for everybody to converge on the surface.

At that moment, as the eastern sky started flooding the convoy with light, there came a frantic shock for the men in *U48*. This was an irritating legacy from an earlier incident when the U-boat Command thought *U26* had been boarded. One of the

precautionary measures taken after that fright was to prevent minelaying boats carrying the same documentation as other boats. Consequently *U48* didn't have the usual G-Square Charts on board and there was no way of communicating the position of the convoy to the other boats. Schultze remained surprisingly calm, but recorded the fact that his superiors needed to think matters through a little more carefully in the future. His main bone of contention was that positions were always transmitted in code, so even if the opposition had a G-Square Chart, the positions wouldn't mean anything to anyone unless they had the radio code as well.

The real crunch came later in the morning, when a call of nature caused 'Vaddi' to ask whether there was a chance for red—this was the colour of the light over the head (lavatory) indicating whether it was empty or engaged. Just at that critical moment, as he illuminated the lamp, the thunderbox was also filled with the shrill of alarm bells. By the time he got back to the control room, he could see *U48* was already plunging down to safer depths. It was a destroyer, coming straight towards them. By the time the distinctive high pitched whine from the propellers faded into nothing, the convoy had gone and the sea was littered with a number of fishing vessels, none of which could be relied upon to be doing what might be expected of them. They could all be anti-submarine hunters and Schultze couldn't take the risk of ignoring them. The opportunity of attacking a convoy had come so quickly and vanished even faster. It was just one of those things. It was war. No one could take anything for certain.

The men in *U48* did succeed in finding some more targets; they suffered another depth-charge attack, although not as devastating as the previous one during an earlier voyage; and they found themselves at the mercy of what appeared to be faulty torpedoes. But by the time it was getting dark on 17 February 1940, they had crossed that barrier of having sunk more than 100,000GRT and this time the Obersteuermann, Willi Kronenbitter, allowed for that minefield by cutting things a bit tighter around the Orkneys and thereby avoiding an unpleasant detour in the German Bight. It was rather good to know that he was steering the most successful boat of World War II—but at that time he didn't know that *U48* was not only the first to reach that 100,000-ton goal, but also remained the most successful boat for the rest of the war.

DEPTH-CHARGE ATTACK

Gus Britton, submariner extraordinary and assistant director of the Royal Navy's Submarine Museum at HMS *Dolphin* until shortly before his death, said, 'I cannot imagine anything worse than being at the receiving end of a depth-charge attack. Once you have endured a few of those, every other frightening experience drops into insignificance.'

After the war, Leading Seaman and radio operator 'Spezi' Henninger and Obersteuermann (navigator) Günther Kautz reconstructed one such depth-charge attack, which occurred in March 1944, while they were in *U471* under Oblt zur See Friedrich Kloevekorn. A dreary four-hour spell, with heavy headphones clamped to his head, was coming to an end and Henninger was pleased that he could wake his team mate to take over from him. There was no need to do this personally, but it was a good excuse to stretch his legs. With another half an hour or so to go until watch change, Henninger returned to his post and wedged his aching body once more in front of the sound detector to listen to the multitude of weird noises produced by the masses of wild life around the boat.

This time, however, there was also a faint unnatural noise. Tension had been high for some time and Kloevekorn was probably on edge like the rest of the crew, but he wasn't showing his anxiety as he lay on his bunk opposite the radio room. There was no

need for Henninger to say anything. It was the way he concentrated on the instrument and the manner in which he twisted the head of the underwater microphones backwards and forwards, but each time returning to the same direction, that suggested that there was something untoward. Gibraltar was close by on the port beam while this irritating high pitched whine was approaching from the opposite direction. It had to be a destroyer. Nothing else was likely to make such distinctive noise.

Henninger held out a spare set of headphones, but Kloevekorn didn't need them. He knew that he could trust his operator. Instead of listening he ordered, 'Crew get ready for action stations. Extreme silence in the boat. There is a destroyer close by.' The word 'destroyer' said it all and was sufficient to prevent men even from coughing. Henninger remarked that there were more than a few concerned glances towards the ceiling as men wondered whether they would get through the narrow strait unscathed.

It wasn't to be. As the whine got louder, a sound like pebbles being thrown at the boat could be heard even without the earphones. This had hardly passed when the pronounced 'ping' of Asdic reverberated through the hull. Then the high pitched whine of the destroyer's turbines increased in volume, suggesting he had gone to a faster speed with a view of dropping depth charges. During those few vital seconds, while the hunter closed in, he was also blind. Both the noise from his own engines and the close proximity to the U-boat rendered his Asdic useless. This was Kloevekorn's chance. He brought the electric motors to top speed and turned away from his original course. It worked. The deafening roar of depth charges was too far away to cause serious damage, although it did hammer the last vestiges of sleep out of the men. As the commotion subsided, the high pitched whine faded with it and *U471*'s engines were instantly switched to silent drive, just fast enough to keep the hydroplanes operational to maintain depth, but hopefully quiet enough not to be heard by the hunter on the surface. This time it didn't help. Although it appeared like an eternity, there were only a few minutes before that distinctive ping from the Asdic reverberated once more through the hull, to be followed by the same routine.

'Depth charges hitting the water,' reported Henninger, taking the headphones off and gripping the edge of the table. The second detonation was terrific. Kloevekorn was on his way from the central control room to the sound compartment, but fell over a mass of tin helmets for the gun crews, which were blasted into the passageway. He cursed briefly before returning to the central control room,

U592

This Blohm und Voss boat from Hamburg was commanded by a son of the city. Kptlt Carl Borm was born there on 10 August 1911, a few years before World War I, and he considered it important to feature the coat of arms (inside the steering wheel) on his boat. The conning tower also had a drawing of the water carrier, who can be seen on the next page. Borm was an unusual character, coming from the battlecruiser *Scharnhorst* and command of torpedo boat *T146*, he returned to large surface ships after his period in *U592*, which was from October 1941 to the end of July 1943. Following this he held several land-based positions before joining the midget weapons unit in Holland and being lucky in surviving the war.

WP=10, S=0, K=50

Above left: *U48* in Kiel with a vast number of success pennants fluttering from the extended periscope. The structure on the top of the conning tower is part of the torpedo loading gear and is usually dismantled when the boat goes to sea. The bulge accommodating the magnetic compass is clearly visible at the base of the conning tower.

hoping it was not necessary to order the clearing of the obstruction. The emergency lighting was producing a ghostly shadowy effect in which it was just possible to determine that a number of the gauges had been smashed and that water was flooding in. Amidst the silent chaos, the intercom sprang reassuringly to life, 'Report damage and absolute silence during repairs.' In films it is necessary to portray such incidents with a good deal of shouting and commotion to make the audience appreciate what is happening, but in reality many of these near death experiences passed off with hardly a voice raised. Everybody was at their station and knew exactly what to do. There was no need to scream and very often it was not even necessary to talk.

Following the detonation, Henninger pushed the earphones back onto his aching head to keep the commander informed about what was happening on the surface. The next attack was not long in coming and was even more ferocious than the previous. The men up top were obviously finding their feet and their target. This time a shattering blast caused the boat to plummet nose first into the depths. 'All spare men to the stern,' rattled through the loudspeakers. Obeying the order was not easy. The passageway was congested with a variety of obstacles dislodged from obscure corners and people were busy replacing fuses, mending leaks and dealing with all manner of temporary repairs. Yet, the emergency lamps provided enough light for staggering aft, while the deep depth gauge indicated quite clearly that *U471* was still descending. The obvious way of stopping such a plunge was to blow the tanks, but that could also give the boat's position away, and it was always questionable whether the upward thrust could be stopped before breaking the surface. Air and the submarine itself expands as the pressure of the surrounding water gets less, therefore there always was a strong chance of such upward movement being converted into an uncontrollable acceleration. These problems are described exceedingly well by Cdr Richard Compton-Hall in his book the *Underwater War 1939–1945*.

Henninger was hardly aware of the boat levelling out and men staggering back to their positions. He was concentrating on a breakdown of his sound detector. There had to be a fault, but he couldn't work out what it was. That high-pitched whine could no longer be heard. The gear had either broken or the bugger was up there waiting for *U471* to give itself away. But despite a few seconds dragging into what appeared to be an eternity, there were no more Asdic pings. Then Henninger realised the reason he couldn't hear anything was because the high pitched whine was running away. Turning up the volume, he

heard it become fainter and fainter. Miracles don't happen very often, but on this occasion their guardian angel was working overtime and a few minutes later there was silence.

U471 quickly returned to its original easterly course and Henninger didn't require another invitation to drop into his bunk. His spell of duty had finished ages ago, but there was still no peace. It was necessary to sleep with a personal respirator. The mouthpiece was uncomfortable and there was no way he could see himself getting any rest with such a cumbrance. Not only was the rubber mouth piece choking him, but the box containing sodium hydroxide for absorbing carbon dioxide was strapped to his chest. Despite the discomfort, Henninger's body wasn't worried about the additional burden, and total exhaustion assured that he quickly dropped into uneasy sleep. He had no idea as to how long he had been lying there, when he was brought to his senses by a powerfully burning sensation on the arm. Picking up the cumbersome container of the breathing apparatus, he realised it had got exceedingly hot. So hot that a large blister had developed on his left lower arm. Henninger jumped up to search for the boat's doctor.

He held the rank of *Obermaat* or Chief Petty Officer and was nothing more than a paramedic, who had been on a first aid course. However, he had proved to everybody on board that he had a natural vocation for dealing with injuries and Obermaat Pietschmann had done more than enough to earn himself the nickname 'Doctor'. During the previous voyage into the North Atlantic, he had demonstrated beyond doubt that he could cope with exceedingly serious injuries and saved more than one life. The blister was comparatively easy to deal with, but left a lasting scar as reminder of the day when Henninger and *U471* stole past the Royal Navy at Gibraltar to break into the fiercely guarded Mediterranean.

There was no way of telling the time inside a submerged U-boat, other than looking at the clock and often the men couldn't be bothered with such a ticking incumbrance. Therefore neither Henninger nor his colleagues had any idea for how long they had been down in the cellar. Only the passing of several duty spells and a number of cold meals indicated that it must have been a long time since the destroyer put in an appearance. Waking from uneasy sleep, Henninger became conscious of sweat running down his face. Among the confusion created by extreme tiredness he heard someone say they had been down for almost 40 hours, but his mind could no longer wrap itself around the comparatively easy figure and it took a while before he realised this was more than

U596

Both Kptlt Gunter Jahn and this Blohm und Voss boat came from Hamburg, whence the unofficial emblem of the water carrier, who served the town before the introduction of piped supplies. Tradition has it that children used to annoy one particular character by shouting '*Hummel, Hummel*' behind his back. His reply, '*Mors, Mors*' (meaning 'Arse, Arse') is not considered offensive by true Hamburgers, who have used this as a greeting ever since. Sadly the custom is slowly dying out. Like Borm of *U592*, Jahn served as commander of a U-boat for only 20 months before taking land-based positions. However he was awarded the Knight's Cross for attacking and at least damaging seven ships. His successor, Oblt zur See Victor-Wilhelm Nonn, managed to hit 10 ships towards the latter part of 1943, quite a remarkable achievement under incredibly difficult circumstances. Oblt zur See Hans Kolbus commanded *U596* for only a few weeks before the boat was destroyed during an air raid in Greece which also killed two of the crew.

WP=13, S=--, K=--

Left: Kpt zur See Robert Gysae wearing the Knight's Cross with Oakleaves. The success pennant in the top left hand corner was for *U177*'s last victim, the 419,5GRT Greek freighter *Efthalia Mari*, sunk in the Indian Ocean on 5 August 1943. During the war, it was a fad for the commander to be the only person on board to wear a white hat.

one and a half days. They had never been down so long before. Peering through the circular doorway in the pressure resistant bulkhead, Henninger watched the engineering officer analyse the foul air. His sarcastic remark that the handbook's statement about life being no longer possible with such a high concentration of carbon dioxide, was easier to comprehend. Henninger could feel the ache in every muscle as he dragged himself to his seat in the sound room. At least he was lucky that he could sit down while on duty.

There was no point in activating any of the radios, but he had to take his turn at the all important sound detector. That was now the only means of knowing what was happening around them. Every muscle in his body ached and Henninger devoted some time to searching for the cause. There had to be more injuries somewhere, but there weren't any. It was just fatigue caused by a shortage of oxygen and breathing too much carbon dioxide. With his mind drifting back to biology lessons at school, Henninger realised that they were all poisoning themselves. Not only that, but the stench from the lavatory combined with an abundance of sweat and oil made him feel sick, but it was only when he found himself lying on the commander's bunk that he realised he was one of the first to have succumbed to the foul air and must have passed out. Even the eau de Cologne which was being wiped around his face did not relieve the pain from the lethargic muscles.

Wondering why the old man was not surfacing, Henninger heard the engineering officer tell Kloevekorn that unless he gave the order to surface soon, there would be no more energy in the system to get up there and another attack could seal their fate. The lethargic reaction of both men, while they tried to conduct a simple conversation, made Henninger realise that officers were just as human as the rest of the crew. Kloevekorn knew that both the men and the machinery had reached their limits. They had been down in the cellar for 48 hours or two full days, but enduring the extreme pain of such supreme sacrifice was better than being sent to their deaths. Kloevekorn probably had been praying that something might destroy them quickly to relieve the agony. He didn't like it either, but had no choice. He had to do his best for his men. Eventually when he did prise the hatch open, he discovered that the pressure inside had increased to such an extent that a wind whisked his cap up onto the conning tower and the suction very nearly impaled him on the locking mechanism of the hatch.

The fresh air brought with it a deluge of radio signals, including the most welcome message that Kloevekorn had been promoted to *Kapitänleutnant*. On top

of this, 'Hobel' Peters, the engineering officer, was handed a tiny brass badge showing the narrows of Gibraltar as birthday present. Once on the surface, *U471* sailed so close to Spain that lookouts reported car headlamps on the coast road. The calmness of the warm Mediterranean spring night had hardly started spreading throughout the stuffy interior when alarm bells shrilled to wake the dead. Once more, *U471* dropped into the depths, but this time the men knew it couldn't be for very long. They had already fought to the last cartridge. All the canisters for the personal breathing gear had been consumed, meaning this next dive was certainly not going to be as long as the last. Sitting anxiously by the sound detector, Henninger could not hear anything. One sweep was followed by another, but there were no sounds. The commander cursed the gear as being useless and when this failed as well, he blamed the operators. Yet, despite all protestations, no one could hear the huge shadow reported by the lookouts. Henninger was still sweeping the gear around when he heard, 'Periscope Depth,' and then, 'Prepare to surface.' Soon afterwards both machinery and radio operators were vindicated. That shadow

turned out to be a three-masted sailing schooner. No wonder its engines could not be heard. A few days later *U471* made fast in its new base of Toulon, to discover that only two from five boats had actually succeeded in that highly dangerous breakthrough into the Mediterranean.

The breathing gear, mentioned by 'Spezi' Henninger, was the so-called Kalipatrone, which consisted of a large tin strapped to the chest, containing sodium hydroxide or potash for absorbing carbon dioxide as it was breathed out. These cumbersome devices were initially the only means for purifying air inside a submerged boat. Later they were replaced by similar cartridges fixed to the walls, but these were not as efficient as the personal devices. Therefore many boats continued to carry these respirators as well as having larger air purification systems fitted to the boat itself. In addition to these, every man was usually issued with a personal respirator, similar to the British Davis Submarine Escape Apparatus. Since the German version was made by the firm with the name Dräger it became known as the 'Dräger Lung', rather than the official name of *Tauchretter* or diving rescuer. It consisted of a large rubber bag which fitted

U598

U598 under Kptlt Gottfried
Holtorf left the headquarters of
the 5th Flotilla shortly after
signing this page at 19:00 in the
evening of 7 July 1942. The men
then took a steadying drink to
calm the nerves and awaited
darkness before venturing out to
sea. The boat was later refuelled
near the Azores and undertook
four arduous missions into the
North Atlantic at a time when it
was becoming exceedingly difficult
to find convoys. Indeed the
majority of boats were coming
home empty handed, but Holtorf
managed to sink two ships and
damage one more before he was
finally caught. However, his end did
not pass without incredible
tension. The boat was so badly
damaged by a Liberator from
VB-107 Squadron, USN that it was
unable to dive and the following
day another Liberator came so
low into an attack that it crashed
as a result of being caught in the
blast of its own depth charges,
killing all 12 of the crew. Yet, this
unexpected momentum of success
did not help the men in *U598*. A
third Liberator from the same
squadron finished off the stricken
U-boat that same day of 23 July
1943.

WP=4, S=2, K=44

around the neck, with most of its bulk
strapped to the man's chest. Inside was a
small cylinder filled with compressed
oxygen rather than air, and a tin for
absorbing carbon dioxide. The idea was
that the person breathes air from the
rubber bag and then a valve forces exhaled
air through the canister to absorb carbon
dioxide. Fresh air contains about 21%
oxygen and hardly any detectable amount
of carbon dioxide, while exhaled air is
made up of 16% oxygen plus just under
5% carbon dioxide. Therefore the Dräger
Lung only needed to add a small quantity
of oxygen towards the mixture in the bag
and made it possible for men to breathe
underwater for about half an hour. The
apparatus could also be inflated to act as a
floatation aid.

Although this sounded very simple,
there were a number of problems and the
following has been included from the log of
U198. The commander, Werner Hartmann,
had been a *Kapitän zur See* for four
months, when he wrote the following. It
was unusual for a person with this rank to
be commanding a submarine, but *U198*
was a massive, very-long-range boat of
Type IXD2, which was due to undertake
voyages to the Far East, where part of the

Above: *U48* with (from left to right)
**Funkgefreiter Waldemar Ischner,
Funkmaat Willi Kruse, Funkoberge-
freiters Kurt Schneegass and Walter
Lang,** who kindly donated a magnificent
collections of photographs of *U48* to
the U-Boot-Archiv while it was still
based at the naval air station at
Westerland on the Island of Sylt.

commander's duties were to negotiate with
Japanese authorities. The log entry is timed
at 22:00 hours on 10 October 1943:

*'We discovered that 63 from a total of 75
Dräger lungs were leaking and therefore
had only a limited use. Some of this
damage was due to punctures which have
been repaired but six are so badly
damaged that we do not have the means of
mending them on board. Following this
discovery, it was decided to check the
lifejackets as well. Shortly before leaving, a
man fell overboard while fuelling and
discovered that he could not inflate his
lifejacket. Since he was wearing heavy
clothing, he only just managed to keep*

U600

One wonders whether the watercolour circles in the background were a mistake. Perhaps Kptlt Bernhard Zurmühlen wanted to insert the coat of arms of the City of Bielefeld, over the top but then decided the background was not good enough. Having been born there meant he probably had stronger than average feelings for the city which had sponsored his boat. He frequented the North Atlantic for over a year during a most difficult period from 14 July 1942 until 25 November 1943 when he and his 53 men in this Type VIIC boat were killed by the frigates **HMS** *Blackwood* and **HMS** *Bazely*.

WP=6, S=0, K=54

Left: The hierarchy of *U48* relaxing on the 'Wintergarden', with 20mm anti-aircraft gun in the foreground. The fact that the men are sporting new Iron Crosses would suggest that this was taken shortly after the outbreak of war, when the winter weather was getting a bit colder. Lt zur See Erich Zürn, the engineer officer on the right, joined the boat for her fifth operational voyage, so this picture could well have been taken during the minelaying voyage to Weymouth on England's south coast. The commander, Herbert Schultze, is wearing a muff for keeping his hands warm and a fur hat. The 1WO, Reinhard ('Teddy') Suhren is on his right and the next person is Otto Ites, the 2WO.

himself afloat. This damage was not noticed before, but suggests that greater care must be taken with the issue and maintenance of these vital pieces of equipment.'

Towards the end of the war, Dräger lungs were used for other ingenious purposes. Since they consisted of an air and watertight bag with a massive seal at the bottom, to enable the oxygen cylinder and the potash container to be replaced, they offered a good hiding place for anything which should not get wet. This was used by men of *U977* to hold some of their private belongings when they were set ashore, before Kptlt Heinz Schäffer undertook his momentous voyage to Argentina after the war. A number of married and engaged men preferred to make their way home instead of accompanying Schäffer on this risky and lengthy undertaking. So, they were set ashore in Norway with reasonable supplies and took their private belongings inside sealed Dräger lungs. However, although well prepared, the plan was frustrated by a low, smooth granite rock. Brushing against it, a number of men were

thrown off the upper deck to end up in the water where they lost their belongings.

'Spezi' Henninger and the men aboard *U471* during that long submerged voyage through the Strait of Gibraltar were lucky because the depth-charge attacks lasted for only a relatively short period and their boat incurred no life-threatening damage to impair progress. *U170*, under Oblt zur See Hans Gerold Hauber, was not let off so easily. This ocean-going Type IXC-40 was schnorkelling homeward off southwest Ireland when the engines were stopped for a periodic search with the underwater sound detector. (Ships still too far away to be seen from the top of the conning tower could often be heard by the hydrophones.) Usually the radio operator was greeted by a multitude of sounds from marine life in the proximity, but on this occasion there were a number of different faint mechanical noises radiating from the same source, suggesting there was something on the move.

The volume increased considerably during the following 30 minutes until it was clear that a number of ships were heading towards *U170*. At around midday,

when Hauber eventually took the boat to periscope depth, he couldn't believe his eyes. He was on his way back from a frustratingly lean operation in the Freetown area of Africa and now this was the second convoy in two days. At least 20 ships were heading straight towards him, presenting such good targets that he planned an attack the rear of the two columns. However, the distinctive thumping of reciprocating engines in the merchantmen was soon accompanied by what sounded like a faint circular saw. It had to be a destroyer. Hauber was not too perturbed and ordered the acoustic torpedo in tube two to be made ready. The tension of the extreme silence in the boat was suddenly interrupted by the announcement that the high pitched whine of a torpedo was approaching exceedingly fast. Quickly it became apparent that the opposition had similar ideas and had already pressed the firing button. Remaining glued to his saddle by the attack periscope inside the conning tower, Hauber calmly ordered the boat down to 80m, allowing the torpedo to pass harmlessly over the top and hopefully head towards the convoy.

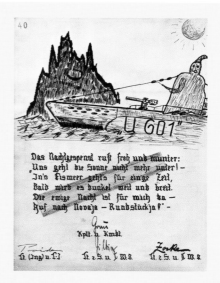

U601

U601 sailed on some eleven war patrols into cold northern waters, but put to sea on no less than 21 occasions—a considerable number of which were commuting from one place to another seeking out repair facilities. The first commander, Kptlt Peter-Ottmar Grau, was a teddy bear with a hard iron core, an essential quality for any successor to the vivacious Engelbert Endrass of **U46**, shortly after he received the Oakleaves for the Knight's Cross. Run-in veteran seamen didn't take kindly to inexperienced new commanders, no matter what high land rank they might hold. Following **U601**, Grau commanded **U872** and **U3015**. **U601**'s second commander, Oblt zur See Otto Hansen, went down with the boat when it was depth-charged by a Catalina from No 210 Squadron, RAF on 25 February 1944.

WP=10 + 4 transport/transit patrols, S=0, K=52

The boat had hardly settled at its new depth when it was shaken so violently that the everybody was thrown into total darkness. Water could be heard pouring in. Hauber couldn't determine where, but knew he could rely on his men to deal with it. The smashed shallow depth gauges looked dramatic, but hardly affected the efficiency of the boat and a stark beam from a dimming torch picked out the deep diving gauge, indicating that the boat was still slowly descending. Although there was plenty of leeway before a critical depth would be reached, the engineering officer ordered a little air to be blown into the tanks to compensate for the downward momentum. The boat was back under control when something hit the upper deck with a loud clang. Whatever it was, it didn't explode, but left the men with the weird feeling that a depth charge might have lodged there, waiting for greater pressure before exploding. Hauber made a mental note not to go any deeper, when the boat dropped down on its own accord. Everybody held their breath. Earlier the engineering officer tried halting the downward movement by engaging the large ballast pump to expel water from the

bilges, but this did not work terribly well. Once again he ordered a little more air to be blown into the tanks. Although the bilge pump was still running, it appeared as if the water was entering faster than it could be expelled. Yet, despite considerable damage, *U170* was left in peace to nurse its wounds for some 10 hours before Hauber felt it was safe enough to surface. The damage report is shown on page 95.

The shrapnel found on the upper deck was too thick to have come from a depth charge, so it seems highly likely that *U170* was attacked with a torpedo. This took place towards the end of October 1944 when the French ports were no longer a viable proposition for U-boats, so *U170* headed north to sail around the top of Britain. A day later, despite the damage, U-boat Command asked Hauber not to forget his weather reports, since these were of vital importance. The men struggled with the damage and, in the end, decided against running into Norway for repairs. Instead *U170* kept going until 4 December 1944 when the men made fast in Flensburg, marking the end of a 126-day or just over four-month long voyage.

Above: Funkmaat WIli Kruse of *U48*, who took many of these photographs.

Far left: *U48*, the most successful boat of World War II, with the 88mm quick-firing deck gun clearly visible. The jumping wire over the men's heads served as radio aerial and anchorage for attaching safety belts when men worked on the upper deck in rough weather.

U170's DAMAGE REPORT

Manometers and main lighting circuits out of order.

On the upper deck

Air supply duct squashed.

Both starboard and port diesel air supply valves are leaking. Schnorkel air supply and exhaust system leaking as well.

Exhaust system torn apart.

The venting system for diving bunker 7 has been torn open.

The schnorkel no longer fits inside the bracket on the top of the conning tower.

A pressure resistant container for rubber dinghy and two munitions containers are torn open or squashed.

The linkage for the seal over the exhaust pipes is bent.

The torpedo aiming device cannot be rotated.

Central Control Room

50% of the water indicators for the trimming system are damaged.

The valves for the trimming system are damaged.

A number of screws holding the trimming system in place have loosened themselves.

The taps in various speaking tubes do not seat properly and are thus leaking.

Magnetic compass is not functioning.

Navigation periscope totally out of action. It is flooded and cannot be raised. The attack periscope is not functioning either.

A number of compressed air bottles are leaking.

Various pipes leading to diving tanks are torn.

The echo sounder does not work.

Diesel Engines

Welding seams in the fuel oil supply valve are cracked.

The port diesel clutch is rattling.

One of the auxiliary fuel pumps is broken.

Auxiliary cooling water pump housing is torn open.

Further damage in the cooling water system and the fuel supply system.

Electric Motors

Rudder indicator, engine telegraph and revolution counter are broken.

Fresh water still is broken.

Some battery switches, both engine telegraphs, the bow hydroplanes and the main rudder were put out of action by the first major detonation but have since been got to work again.

U605

U605 was commanded by Herbert-Viktor Schütze, who should not be confused with Viktor Schütze of *U19*, *U11*, *U25*, *U103* and later chief of the 2nd U-Flotilla in Lorient. Herbert-Viktor made an auspicious start with U-boats, sinking three ships during his first three war patrols, but he was hunting not only at more difficult times than his namesake but his boat was also sent to a considerably more inhospitable area off Algiers, where it was caught by a Hudson bomber from No 233 Squadron, RAF on 28 July 1942 and was sunk with depth charges during an efficient, swift kill.

WP=3, S=0, K=46

Left: Mechanikerobergefreiter Hans Bauer of *U48* wearing a coat without lapels as issued to technical staff. Seamen had coats with large lapels.

On Far-Flung Oceans

Although a large number of war correspondents and photographers were given honorary commissions, very few of them were officers in their own right. Walter Schöppe was one of this rare breed, a journalist who was also a fully fledged naval officer. In consequence of this, he was pushed into a number of horrendous assignments. He participated in what was thought at the time to be a suicide mission— the Channel Dash of the *Gneisenau* and *Prinz Eugen* from Brest north through the Channel under the very noses of the British. He photographed the proceedings from the heavy cruiser *Prinz Eugen*, producing a unique record of the trip. One of his most hard-hitting pictures shows the guns of the *Prinz* at sunrise in the Elbe estuary with the caption, 'When we left Brest we all thought that we would not be alive to see this sight.'

Schöppe later boarded *U178*, a very-long-range boat, for a voyage into the Indian Ocean and from there, unexpectedly, on to Penang and Singapore in Malaya. His chronicles are of special interest because they describe the punishing life inside the U-boat, something which tends to be omitted from official logs. The discomforts endured by the men were taken for granted and even serious injuries were usually not mentioned. Also of great interest are his comments about personal relationships under staggeringly difficult, cramped and stuffy conditions. He goes to some lengths to explain the feelings of the men and to mention the arguments which raged in various quarters, especially the disagreements between the commander— Kpt zur See Hans Ibbeken—and his officers.

The boat is of special interest. This very-long-range design of Type IXD2 was created by enlarging a standard Type IX. The hull was only some 10cm wider, but it had an additional section in the stern with a second set of engines and this was balanced with another accommodation compartment forward of the conning tower. Since it was double-hulled, the fuel bunkers were wrapped around the outside of the pressure hull, and this meant that these tanks were exceptionally large and could provide a staggering range of more than 32,000 nautical miles or 60,000km. This was a fantastic improvement on a standard Type IXC, which could cover only about half that distance.

However, the modifications also produced a number of disadvantages. The majority of the fittings were similar to the standard type, meaning that the hydroplanes were less effective. Keeping this extra bulk at periscope depth without bows and stern breaking the surface was indeed a major problem. In addition to this, it was more sluggish and took a considerably longer time to dive—so these huge monstrosities were not cut out for areas where they were likely to be surprised by fast-flying aircraft. Consequently the cumbersome whale was unsuitable for the bitter convoy war in the North Atlantic, and so had to be used away from this arena, in oceans where anti-submarine forces were likely to be less experienced and, therefore, slower.

U178 was commissioned by Kpt zur See Hans Ibbeken on 14 February 1942 and left Kiel for its first war voyage on 8 September of the same year, with three highly contrasting characters in the leading positions. Hans Ibbeken often boasted that he was the oldest U-boat Commander, although this was not true. He was born on 20 September 1899 and the 'Wild Moritz'— Georg von Wilamowitz-Moellendorf, who commanded *U2* and *U459*, was born on 7 November 1893. Korvkpt Leo Wolfbauer, commander of *U463*, served as watch officer aboard *U29* during World War I and was born on 21 July 1895, only 24 years after the founding of the German nation. Although Hans Ibbeken contributed some far-sighted planning, such as asking a professor of music to compile a grand collection of records with calming melodies, it quickly it became apparent that he lacked the determination, consideration and integrity for such a demanding post. Despite his seniority, it wasn't easy for him to get away with his numerous shortcomings and it often came to fierce exchanges of words with the first watch officer, Oblt zur See Wilhelm Spahr, and the most capable engineering officer, Kptlt (Ing) Hans Gottwald. Ibbeken also flung his venom at other crew members, but the lower ranks were hardly in a position to protest.

Spahr has been described as a passionate sailor who never let anyone down, broke his word or get terribly excited about unexpected problems. He reached his position in *U178* by demonstrating that he

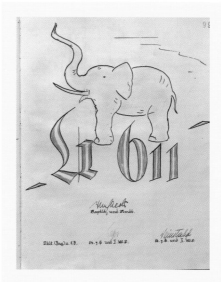

U611

The elephant featured on the conning tower as well as on this page of the visitors' book. In December 1942, *U611*, under Kptlt Nikolaus von Jacobs, was supplied in mid-Atlantic by *U460* just a few days before the elephant was sunk by a Liberator from VP-84 Squadron, USN. Lookouts aboard the corvette *Potentilla*, escorting convoy HX217 to the south of Iceland, watched the aircraft (Sqn Ldr T. M. Bullock, who also destroyed *U514* and *U597*) dive before seeing and hearing the depth-charge detonations. Racing over to the spot, the Royal Navy found the seas empty. The explosions had already done their job and sent all 45 men aboard the U-boat to the bottom.

WP=1, S=0, K=45

Left: Maschinenmaat (Engine Petty Officer) Rudi Ohlheiser of *U178* wearing submarine escape apparatus for a dive to inspect the exterior of the boat, while Matrosenobergefreiter Karl Huruck holds the lifeline.

Time dragged by exceedingly slowly, and long before the homeward voyage was started, everybody on board agreed that they would not sail a second time with 'Ibbo'. This nickname may not sound derogatory, but the way it was spoken immediately classed it among those words smeared on public lavatory walls. Many of his actions, such as not diving at sundown or sunup, when it is virtually impossible to spot an approaching aircraft against the glaring light, chain-smoking at night on the bridge and not pursuing targets with the necessary determination made him a most unwelcome person on board. Yet, despite numerous disagreements, U178 returned to Bordeaux after a staggering 123 days at sea.

'Ibbo' would not take U178 out again. He was replaced by a formidable character, with a Knight's Cross hanging around his neck. Korvkpt Wilhelm Dommes learned his trade in U431, mainly in the punishing conditions of the Mediterranean. But it was not only 'Ibbo' who left—a good number of other men moved on to further training courses and then promotion in other submarines.

Hans Gottwald was promoted to become an engineering officer on the staff of the Flag Officer for U-boats in Italy and was succeeded by another remarkable individual, Kptlt (Ing) Karl-Heinz Wiebe, who was later awarded the Knight's Cross. At his arrival, Walter Schöppe said of him:

'With 628 war days at sea, he has got to be one of the most experienced engineers in the navy. His first voyage with U178 was also his 13th aboard a U-boat—but it would be the most difficult of all. U178 fought in the immense heat of the Indian Ocean, where temperatures soared and with the humidity as high as 91%. Under these conditions, when it was punishingly hot to move, Wiebe set about reconditioning the engines by fitting new pistons. What is more, he took up the post aboard U178 knowing that the boat had not been through a major overhaul and was therefore likely to develop a number of serious breakdowns.'

Sadly, the jovial petty officer Hermann Mayer also had to leave U178 due to ear damage which made it difficult for him to hear and thus rendered him unfit for further U-boat duties. He became an instructor with a training establishment.

It was Sunday, 28 March 1943, a dull, drizzly day, when U178 nosed out of Bordeaux, to negotiate the Gironde and then find a safe way through the Bay of Biscay. Large, fast-flying aircraft had already become a major threat and everybody on board was pleased to join the protection of a small convoy heading west. U178 had long left this group, but had not gone too far, when the radio announced the sinking of an Italian ship and gave orders

was a most able warrant officer, who remained cool under the severest fire. On top of this, he had the rare ability of being able to boost the morale of flagging mates, even under the most daunting conditions. He had joined the navy as an ordinary sailor and then worked his way up to become a warrant officer at a time when this training was the most intense and even more comprehensive than that given to potential commissioned officers. At the beginning of the war he was the *Obersteuermann* or navigator in *U47* under the legendary Kptlt Günther Prien. It was Spahr who directed the boat into the Royal Navy's anchorage at Scapa Flow to sink the battleship HMS *Royal Oak*.

The friction among the leadership was not the only worry. U178 had been at sea for over a month and was further south than any U-boat had ever travelled before when it was discovered that the fitting-out flotilla in Kiel had somehow miscalculated the provisions: there was not enough food on board. This, incidentally, was not that unusual, although the 5th Flotilla was not responsible for all the shortcomings. For example, at the beginning of the war, *U35* under Kptlt Fritz-Julius Lemp found that tins of bread contained evaporated milk instead. In May 1937, while participating as a unit of an international peace keeping force off Spain, *U26* under Korvkpt Werner Hartmann found that some provisions were labelled with a 'use-by-date' of January 1937. The shortage of food aboard *U178*

was made even worse by Ibbeken's lack of enthusiasm for pursuing targets. Instead of making an effort to attack, he allowed a number of large merchant ships and tankers to slip away, which infuriated the crew. The temperature inside the stuffy pressure hull was often more than 38°C during the day, making pure survival a painful activity and any form of physical activity torturous.

With men confined in cramped accommodation, small things started irritating people and insignificant irregularities led to ferocious arguments. It was necessary to introduce some variation into the monotonous schedules, and this gave rise to some ingenious projects. When the engineering officer discovered that the engines were consuming considerably more fuel than anticipated, Wilhelm Spahr and Oberbootsmaat Hermann Meyer discussed the possibility of rigging up sails. Apparently it had worked during World War I and could now help U178 out of the rather nasty predicament. A number of canvas mattress covers were collected, sewn into an improvised sail and rigged up on the forward periscope. The astonishing thing was that this improvisation worked without bending the periscope and the boat managed one and a half knots (almost 3km/hr) with the engines on stop. However, having proved the point, it was decided that this was also rather a conspicuous advertisement and likely to be spotted by the enemy, so the scheme was abandoned.

U627

The keel for this Type VIIC was laid down at Blohm und Voss in Hamburg on 7 August 1941. It was launched on 29 April 1942 and commissioned by Kptlt Robert Kindelbacher on 18 June of that year. Trials and training lasted for just over three months and then, on 15 October 1942, the boat left the 5th Flotilla in Kiel. Less than two weeks later it was lying on the bottom of the North Atlantic towards the southwest of Reykjavik in Iceland. All 44 men inside died when the boat was depth-charged by an aircraft from No 206 Squadron, RAF.

WP=1, S=0, K=44

for several boats to search for survivors. None was found, although an abundance of wreckage, some unused lifejackets and a few empty rescue rafts indicated that something untoward had happened.

Not long after leaving this devastation, lookouts spotted a small convoy and Dommes immediately placed himself in front of the potential targets. Reporting the news to the Operations Room produced the unexpected response to keep shadowing until U-Mohr made contact with the merchant ships. The wording made it plain that Dommes was not to risk his floundering whale and that he was to continue with his voyage into the South Atlantic and Indian Ocean. It was still light when the radio announced that *U124*, under the newly promoted Korvkpt Johann Mohr, had sighted the convoy. The news had hardly spread when lookouts spotted the tiny black streak sneaking into a

favourable attacking position for the coming night. Had the convoy not been within sight as well, Wiebe would have persuaded Dommes to creep up on Mohr, to congratulate his old commander on his two-day-old promotion. But it was war and not even safe to use a signal lamp, so *U178* followed its orders to vanish over the southern horizon. Darkness had hardly settled in when a multitude of detonations filled the air and an abundance of starshells illuminated the black sky to make it look almost like a brilliant white day. Then, suddenly there was silence. The explosions ceased, the ether went quiet and Mohr didn't respond to requests for his position. It wasn't hard to guess what had happened.

Mohr had joined this famous Type IXB boat as Second Watch Officer, in September 1940, three months after it had been commissioned by Kptlt Georg-Wilhelm Schulz and remained on board long enough

Above left: The saying 'Only another 60 days?' from *U178* became famous enough to feature on the conning tower together with a portrait of a dreaded cockroach, which troubled the men so much in the Indian Ocean. This shows the boat under Kptlt Wilhelm Spahr, coming back into Bordeaux after its momentous voyage to the Indian Ocean.

Far left: Some adjustments are needed to the side of *U178* and Zentraleobermaschinist Hermann Matzat, with lifejacket, is secured by a thin rope while he tightens some screws below the upper deck. It is remarkable is that he is still fully clothed and wearing a cap.

to become 1WO. In July 1941, he went off to commanders' school but was back in September to take charge of the highly successful boat. The fact that he gained both the Knight's Cross and the Oakleaves indicates that his achievement followed along the same lines as those established by Schulz, whose photograph has appeared in a multitude of postwar books, although many captions state that the picture shows Herbert Schultze of *U48*.

Karl-Heinz Wiebe sat in profound depression. His second U-boat war voyage had been with Mohr. That was one of those visits to the Cape Hatteras area of the United States early in 1942, when the hunting was still exceptionally good: they had returned home with one of the biggest bags ever achieved by a submarine. Dommes was also subdued, blaming himself for luring Mohr to his death. Had he not sent that stupid sighting report, then Mohr and his men would still be alive. It was moments like these when one suddenly noticed how empty the world was becoming and how lonely it could be, even when surrounded by a good colleagues. The depression was not allowed to last long and a constant stream of training exercises diverted the men's thoughts. With a number of new faces, it was necessary to go through all the procedures until every action was more than perfect. Dommes knew the only way that they would survive was to go through the entire training repertoire, to assure that nothing was left to chance.

It was during the evening of 9 April 1943 that a grinding noise in the starboard shaft suggested something was amiss. As a result engines were stopped and the boat dropped down to a safe depth for repairs to be put in hand. This took a painful 20 hours and although it occupied only a small number of men, the rest remained apprehensive. It was not a pleasant feeling to know that one of the major powerplants wasn't working. Bearing in mind that this major repair became necessary after just 21 days at sea, it was not a terribly good omen for what might follow. Once again, these thoughts had hardly been chewed through when they were derailed by lookouts reporting a submarine on the surface. Luckily it responded to a German recognition signal and turned out to be *U509* under Kptlt Werner Witte, on its way back to France. Both boats came close enough together to exchange some tools, signal books and a little fresh food. *U509* had been at sea since the day before Christmas Eve of the previous year, making any contribution to the by now monotonous menu of preserved food most welcome.

From then on the monotony of life inside a small iron tube developed an atmosphere where time lost its significance. Dommes continued practising for every emergency he could imagine, but even that became second nature and the men didn't

have to think about it anymore. Instead they performed the complicated routines as reflex actions, sometimes not even bothering to wake up properly. The crossing of the line— or Equator—was celebrated in true naval fashion with the old lags providing the most horrendous treatment for the dirty newcomers, who needed to be cleaned before they could enter Neptune's realm. However, the celebrations were interrupted. Maschinenmaat Rudi Ohlheiser had to go swimming with a lifeline and submarine escape apparatus to repair a leak in one of the external tanks.

The next stages of the voyage can be described by a few extracts from Walter Schöppe's journal:

'Further work was necessary on the outside of the diving tanks and in addition to this there was a noticeable oil trail in our wake. This meant considerable effort was needed to saw through pipes, cleaning them out by squirting high pressure water through and then welding them shut again … During this most monotonous voyage to our operations area, two additional men were allowed on the bridge for smoking … Sailing around the southern reaches of Africa was an apprehensive period because during the first voyage, a few months earlier, lookouts had spotted five mines laid some time earlier by the auxiliary cruiser Atlantis *under Kpt zur See Bernhard Rogge. On the one hand we didn't want to go on too long a detour further south, but on the other we didn't want to bump into one of these either … This oil in our wake has become a real problem. Whatever is done, it doesn't seem to go away. Consequently the atmosphere inside the boat is not too good … Now where we are closer to land we find that there are a good number of aircraft about, and vigilance is of utmost*

U659

U659 sailed on five war patrols under Kptlt Hans Stock, sinking one ship and damaging three more, before coming to a rather unusual end. Hunting a convoy off Cape Finisterre the lookouts failed to spot *U439* under Oblt zur See Helmut von Tippelskirch converging on the same target. The boats collided, tearing holes in each other's pressure hull and sank rapidly. Although the convoy escorts, and probably the lookouts aboard the U-boats, were concentrating on the burning ships in the convoy, Royal Navy lookouts noticed the crash and were able to rescue three men from *U659* and nine from *U439*.

WP=5, S=3, K=44

importance... We had several chances of getting within shooting distances of targets, but every time something prevented Dommes from driving home the attack. This time the torpedo mechanic failed to get the tubes open and the ship turned away before the order "fire" could be given. It's pure frustration. Later, one ship actually stopped the moment the torpedoes were fired, suggesting it had some kind of ultrasensitive sound detectors. It avoided our salvo by going hard astern. Six torpedoes were shot but not a single one brought it to a standstill before it vanished into Portuguese territorial waters and then, to make matters worse, we were attacked by an aircraft. It was not pleasant and most frustrating.

'We have now been at sea for 69 days and at last succeeded in damaging a ship. One of the torpedoes missed or didn't explode and it looks as if the target had

sufficient life left to get away. [Jürgen Rohwer's *Axis Submarine Successes* suggest that this was the 6,586GRT Dutch freighter *Salabangka*, which sank a few days later while under tow.] *... The problem with this massive boat is that it is very difficult to control, especially during submerged attacks, and once the sea gets rougher than Force 4 it is virtually impossible to maintain periscope depth without parts of the hull also breaking through the surface of the water. The other problem is that turning at periscope depth is virtually impossible. The boat lurches around so slowly that it can hardly keep up with the speed of a slow merchantman. If we remain on the surface, we must expect aircraft attacks and this could make matters considerably worse because of the long diving time. On top of all this, it is extremely difficult to find the enemy on the vastness of this never-ending ocean, but the*

Above left: Refuelling at sea was the weakest link in many far-off U-boat operations and the Allies made a concerted effort to eliminate this vital supply system. Specially built supply submarines appeared during 1942, but they were quickly hunted down and there were so few that other large boats were employed for this purpose. This shows *U116* from *U406* during one of those critical refuelling moments. The box-shaped protrusion on top of the bows of *U116* indicates that this is a minelayer of Type XB, the largest German submarine of World War II.

radar detector is active enough to suggest that we are surrounded by masses of hunting aircraft, making life most uncomfortable.

'Those on board who can manage a little elementary mathematics worked out that we were getting through our fuel and it must soon be time to turn round to go home again. The fact that our fuel will only last for another 60 days brought new life into the lethargic reactions of the men … Then on 9 June we received the news that we were due to meet a supply ship, as well as several other U-boats. Still, the saying "only sixty days to go" remained in active circulation … Another normal day rules our lives: Test dives, artillery maintenance and shooting a few rounds to see that the guns are working. This time a routine check disclosed that one of the diesels was leaking somewhere—that irritating oil trail has reappeared—and torpedoes from the outside containers were loaded into the boat. This is always quite a critical period because it means that the boat is not ready for diving and thus a sitting target for anything which happens to be passing.

'On 22 June 1943 we met the tanker Charlotte Schliemann in naval square KR9922. Although the refuelling was strenuous and involved a complete restacking of virtually everything inside the U-boat, there were brief opportunities to go aboard the supply ship for a most welcome change of faces and different news. The auxiliary cruiser Atlantis was sunk on 22 November 1941 while acting as submarine supply ship. At that crucial moment, the commander of U126 [Kptlt Ernst Bauer] was on board, having a shower. Consequently, Dommes was apprehensive about allowing men aboard the supply ship … Dommes became quite seriously ill, complaining of severe stomach pains, and Wilhelm Spahr stood in for him as well as doing his usual jobs. It quickly became apparent that he was far worse than we first thought and it also became apparent that he was suffering from severe depression. I think the main problem was that his earlier experiences in the Mediterranean had robbed him of his mental strength. At one point he even muttered that we will never return from this voyage and both Wiebe and Spahr had strong words with him that he must not make such declarations where the men can hear him.

'It was becoming apparent that the meeting with Charlotte Schliemann had also introduced a number of unwanted stowaways in the form of cockroaches. These tiny insects tended to shy away from light and bred exceedingly fast in our humid, hot atmosphere. Quickly, they became a hated pest, making them more than a mere nuisance. They crawled over sleeping men and, without waking them,

chewed bits of skin, leaving painful, raw patches. Hunting these little offenders with a variety of self-made traps became one of the main pastimes, but all these efforts hardly reduced the total number.

'On 16 July 1943 at 04:00 hours lookouts spotted a shadow in square KE2738. This turned out to be the 6,692GRT freighter City of Canton, which was sunk, but once again there were several torpedo failures. Later, one white man was discovered in a lifeboat among a group of Asians.

'We had only one torpedo left, meaning there was no choice other than head for home, and it was good practice to hit the enemy harder by capturing its key personnel, so we took Reginald Harry Broadbent (Second Officer) prisoner. Obviously he didn't like the prospect, but had no choice. His tropical kit was wet and dirty when he came on board and a number of our men gave him clothes from their own private stock. He was a congenial fellow, who quickly endeared himself sufficiently for Wilhelm Spahr to take him on lookout duty. Harry was astonished to discover that the German binoculars he was using were a good deal better than the standard British issue. He knew full well that it was in his interest to report aircraft quickly because if he did not, he was likely to die with the rest

of us. He found it hard to adapt to the stuffy air inside the boat and occasionally complained at the shortage of cigarettes. Apparently he was used to smoking 50–60 a day. That's about one every ten minutes.

'At 13:30 hours of 1 August 1943 in square JK5282 we got one of those unusual radio messages to refuel a large Italian submarine, the Torelli. It would appear that it was on its way east with a number of German war secrets on board and was now in a position of surrendering these to the Allies. Mussolini had fallen and the Italians had changed sides, to complicate matters considerably. It was important to provide the Torelli with the resources to continue the journey to the Far East rather than run into a nearer British base.

'The refuelling proved to be quite a problem because we had only about 40–50 metres of fire hose and the weather was hardly encouraging for such complicated manoeuvre. In the end it became necessary to transfer our engineering officer [Wiebe] to Torelli to help make a coupling device to join each other's hoses. Even so, the distance between the two boats was still too short for comfort and, to make matters worse, the rough seas prevented us from getting Wiebe back. Consequently he was marooned on the Italian side for a few days until he struck

U704

In addition to the 5th U-Flotilla in Kiel, *U704* passed through six other flotillas, had five commanders, sailed on three war patrols, and returned with technical problems on two occasions shortly after having left. The boat was finally withdrawn from active service in Königsberg, in the eastern Baltic, to serve as training ship, which explains the high number of commanders and flotillas. The boat's war patrols under Kptlt Horst Kessler, who later commanded *U985*, took the boat to St Nazaire, La Pallice, the North Atlantic and Norway.

WP=5, S=--, K=--

Above left: *U571* during a refuelling at sea.

Left: During the refuelling of *Torelli*, *U178*'s engineering officer, Kptlt (Ing) Karl-Heinz Wiebe, was stranded aboard an Italian submarine for several days by exceedingly rough weather. He eventually returned by converting a diving suit into a floating shuttle by inflating it and allowing himself to be pulled back.

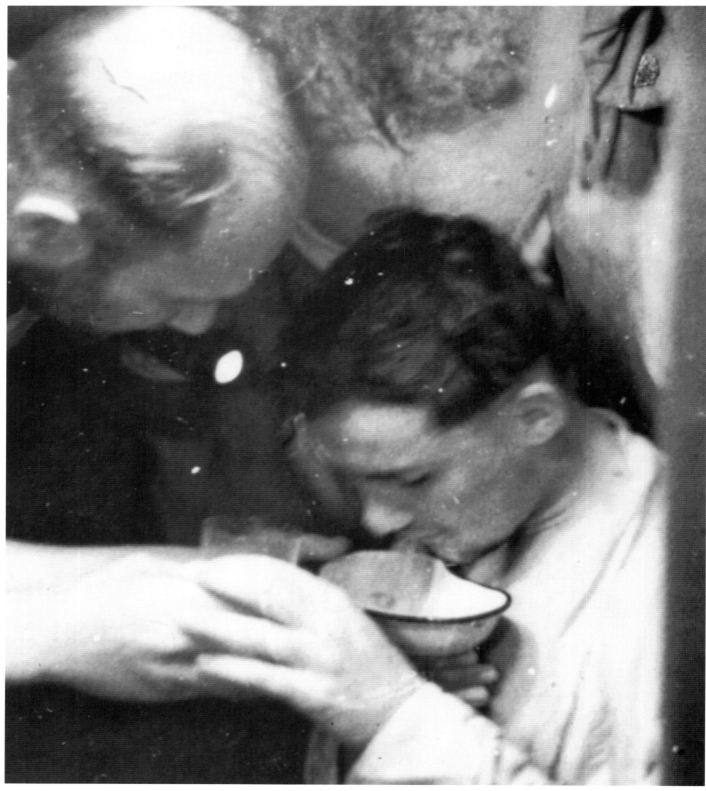

upon the idea of inflating his diving suit like a beach ball and floating back on his own, rather than going in an inflatable. This ingenious idea was still quite dangerous because we did not have a really strong enough rope on board to pull him back.

'The drama with the refuelling had hardly been completed when we were hit by another bombshell. There came one of those "for officer only" radio messages asking Dommes whether it was possible for him to reach Penang in the Far East rather than attempt a return voyage to France. This request wasn't kept secret for long and we didn't know what to think. On the one hand the Far East conjured up visions of paradise, but it was also the unknown and a hell of a long way from home.

'Dommes replied that the crew was generally in quite good shape, but there were several more serious illnesses on board and he could not guarantee that these people would be able to make a return journey if hospitals at the destinations could provide better treatment than the meagre facilities on board.

'Finally, after some consultation and considerable thought, Dommes agreed and turned the boat round to make for Malaya, where U178 arrived on 27 August 1943, after having been at sea for exactly one day short of five months. This in itself was a most staggering performance of endurance, deprivation and making do with the barest of essentials for life.'

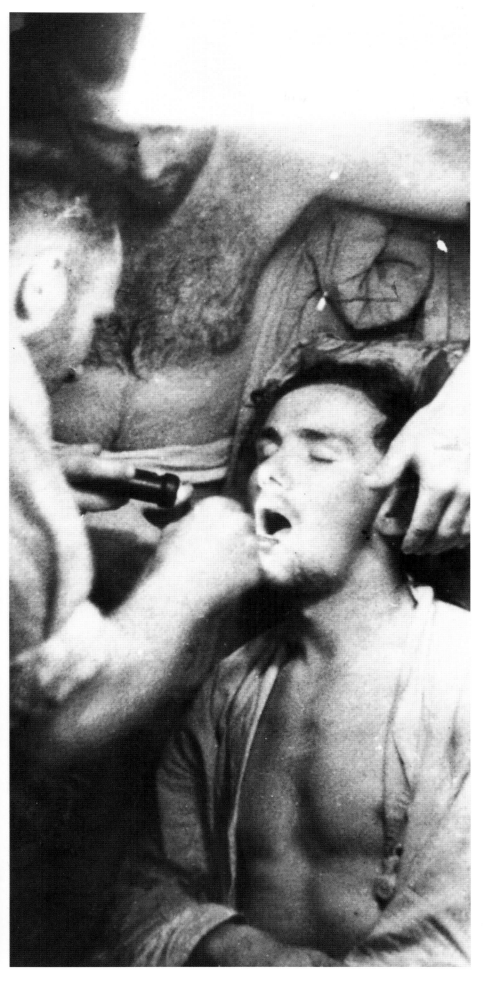

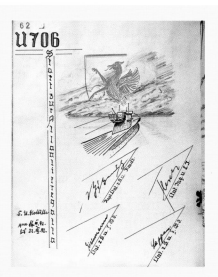

U706

U706 was built by the small Stülken Werft in Hamburg and commissioned on 16 March 1942 by er Kptlt Alexander von Zitzewitz, who was born in Kassel near the Eder Reservoir, whose dam was breached by No 617 Squadron, RAF with Barnes Wallis's famous bouncing bomb. Making for La Pallice as main base, *U706* sailed on six war patrols, although two of them were broken off immediately after leaving port due to mechanical problems. Sinking three ships, this was one of the more successful U-boats. The words running down the page say, 'Start of the Atlantic Regatta.'

WP=6, S=4, K=43

Left and Far left: Men usually underwent a medical before and after each voyage, but even with such stringent checks, there were plenty of opportunities for painful illnesses to develop, especially during the long voyages. Since it was impossible to equip boats for every eventuality, improvisation became the order of the day. This shows emergency dental work being carried out aboard *U178*, during a voyage into the Indian Ocean.

Escape from Occupied France

There are times when not only the unexpected, but also the seemingly improbable turns up in the U-boot-Archiv. Finding some most implausible anonymous reminiscences about *U548's* escape from Lorient to Norway, I asked Horst Bredow whether he knew the name of the author. Glancing at the report, he remembered the face of the person who brought it, but with hundreds of visitors per week, could not recall the name. However, he did confirm the report's authenticity. Shortly afterwards we came across another version of the same account, but this time also with copies of the original logbook and an acknowledgement to the first watch officer, Horst Günther. We succeeded in tracing him and thus identified the author as Heinz Fritsch, who died a few years ago.

Horst Günther also supplied some additional information to go with Fritsch's recollection of this unusual episode of suffering, and we have added a few extra explanations to make Heinz Fritsch's account easier to understand. The incredible point about Fritsch's work is that it describes what happened, but hardly mentions the appalling conditions inside the U-boat nor the suffering endured by those who took part.

'While waiting for lunch during the third week of digging anti-tank ditches around the north of Lorient, a dispatch rider arrived with the instructions to take me to headquarters on the back of his motorbike. It was 10 August 1944. The Normandy landings of D-Day were already history and we were preparing for an onslaught on the landward side. As far as we knew, there were only a few damaged U-boats in port, but no crews and most of the town had been reduced to rubble by incessant air raids, therefore it was difficult to work out why we were still defending the base with such vigour. After all, the large German garrison was cut off, surrounded and doomed into starvation. The driver told me to hold on tight and then manoeuvred his machine through the wildest of terrain, hardly making an effort to avoid ditches, pot holes and the occasional bursts of gunfire and dramatic detonations. Arriving at the massive bunker was somewhat daunting. There had been a considerable change since I left my last U-boat. The large number of massive craters, together with a

forlorn air of abandonment suggested that life was rapidly being squeezed out of the Germany's largest naval base on the Biscay coast.

'Reporting to the appropriate office, I exchanged my pistol and field grey uniform for a tropical outfit. I was not likely to go anywhere hotter than Lorient, but the navy

didn't have any other stocks to hand. Then I was allocated a room and told that I was going to form part of a new U-boat crew. This sounded rather alarming and mysterious, but also exciting because it offered an opportunity to escape from the surrounded mousetrap. The frightful point about the proposition was that the majority

U757

This boat was built by the Naval Dockyard in Wilhelmshaven and commissioned by Kptlt Friedrich Deetz on 28 February 1942 during such cold weather that the brass band could not play because their instruments had frozen and there was a danger of the men getting frostbite from the cold metal. Nevertheless, everything went well and the boat finally sailed into the North Atlantic and later as far south as Freetown in Africa. Yet the gremlins seem to have maintained residence in the machinery because *U757* was forced back into port with mechanical problems on no fewer than seven occasions.

WP=6, S=0, K=49

of others, who had tried this before hadn't get very far and were still lying at the bottom of the Bay of Biscay. But then I was given no choice. It was an order and we had been brought up not to question authority.

'It was during the morning of the following day when I was allowed into Keroman III to report to U584. The first watch officer, Oblt zur See Horst Günther, seemed pleased to see me and said I should report to the chief petty officer, Kurt Weidner, who instructed me to leave my spare set of underwear and two pairs of socks somewhere and then help with the unloading of stores. Going to sea and unloading provisions was more than an enigma, making a number of us wonder why a boat, obviously ready to put to sea, should have the majority of its vital provisions removed. The answer was not

long in coming. It became apparent that some of the crew had gone home on leave and were now cut off by the advancing Allied armies, making their return to Lorient impractical. So, it was a case of collecting together a mishmash of qualified people to take the boat to the crew. The only plus point of this crazy idea was that this hazardous undertaking was going to be an exceedingly brief affair. Indeed, it was just a short and simple task of breaking through the blockade and sailing the short distance of about 500km south to Bordeaux, which was still relatively free of enemy constriction. If we were lucky we could get there in a week's time, but things were unlikely to go smoothly, so we needed to count on ten days or a fortnight.

'The boat was on the verge of leaving, but it still was not known who was going to

Above left: The hinged schnorkel of *U889* lying in the lowered position under the upper deck planking. On the left, the grid in the deck has been raised, while the open circular hatch cover in the pressure hull is visible. Some boats had wooden deck planking, while others had all metal grating. Both were slatted with numerous slots to allow air and water to wash into the space between the upper deck and the pressure hull.

Far left: The schnorkel in its raised position with head valve at the top to prevent water washing down the pipe. It hinged at the bottom and could be lowered into the deck casing when not in use. Air was sucked in through the top while diesel exhaust gasses were expelled through the lower nose.

Right: *U548*'s engineering officer, Oblt zur See (Ing) Josef Stürzinger, and commander, Kptlt Günther Pfeffer, in Holefjord (Norway). Stürzinger was on board during the following voyage when the boat was sunk with all hands, but Pfeffer survived by being ordered to hand over his temporary command to Oblt zur See Erich Krempl.

Below: *U959* was commissioned by Oblt zur See Martin Duppel and was later commanded by Oblt zur See Friedrich Weitz. This shows the starboard 20mm twin anti-aircraft gun, aft of the conning tower. These more powerful guns were installed on enlarged gun platforms from 1942 onwards.

command it or even if there was still such a qualified officer in the base. However, the arrival of a number of officials with an array of heavy packages suggested that U548 was going to carry a considerable cargo as well as passengers, some of whom looked very prim and proper, as if they had never set foot inside a submarine and had no idea of the filthy conditions they were about to endure. The authorities scraped almost an entire crew together. A number of positions were duplicated while others remained vacant, but there was enough expertise to cover this vacuum. In all we had a crew of 54 plus 29 passengers, making a total of at least 83—and remember it was a tight fit to get in a normal crew of 44. U548 was a standard ocean-going Type IXC/40 with a little more room than the Type VIIC, but it was still on the suicidal side of overfull. To describe these conditions, where it was hardly possible to move or stand up, as chaotic would be a coarse understatement.

'The new commander, who arrived only a short time before departure, was Kptlt Günther Pfeffer, a 31-year-old from Dresden with a good saturation of experience aboard U170. This was, luckily, a similar type to U548, but that hardly mattered. It was unlikely that he was going to press any buttons, turn wheels or move levers, so a calm, experienced submariner from any type of boat was very much preferred to a hot-headed, self-professed expert with a "sore throat". [Meaning that he was yearning after a Knight's Cross.]

'Pfeffer appeared without illusions of grandeur and told us that he was going to do his best to take us the short distance to Bordeaux, but whether we would arrive there was going to depend on our efficiency and a bit of luck. He also said, "If we don't know each other now, we'll certainly be a bit better acquainted by the time we get there." Going to sea with such a hotchpotch of men, who had not been together long enough to fuse into a team, must have been somewhat frightening for him. After all, he didn't even know whether we would execute his orders fast enough or correctly. In many ways our venture was a formula for doom, but we didn't look at it in that way at the time. We were pleased for an opportunity of escaping from the mousetrap.

'I manned the hydroplanes in the central control room, making it possible to get first-hand knowledge of what was going on, but the news wasn't terribly encouraging. Progress was slow, a number of high-pitched turbine whines made us change course and then, when all was quiet, we had that tricky task of raising the schnorkel to recharge the batteries without surfacing. Luckily, the hot weather over France extended far out into the Bay of Biscay to calm those naturally turbulent waters.

'Progress was slow. We managed some 59 nautical miles per day at best, often much less, and the presence of both friendly and enemy minefields meant we had to move a good distance away from land, before turning to run south in a long loop. This was going reasonably well, although our passengers seemed to be suffering, when a signal was picked up. It said quite simply, "Pfeffer cancel order to proceed to Bordeaux. Zimmermann has not arrived. Change course and make for Norway. Report position when you are 300 miles from land."

'Eberhard Zimmermann was the appointed commander of U548. He had been cut off in Germany, but no one told us why he couldn't get to Bordeaux. There were no secrets in the boat and the new course of action was openly discussed in the central control room, which was about the only place that was not full of obstructing bodies. Of course, the biggest problem was that the provisions had been unloaded to make way for cargo and passengers, and there was no way that we could start eating them! Therefore it was necessary to devise some feasible plan of drastically reducing rations. We had plenty of rice, noodles and dried potatoes, so the cook conjured up monotonous soups with only a smattering of flavour. It wasn't brilliant, but just had to do. To make matters even worse, no one on board had any idea as to how long this little jaunt was going to take. We knew where Norway was. A few of us had even been there, but there were too many variables to work out how long such a voyage would take. The strange thing is, that none of us ever doubted that we would get there.

'The next problem came from the engineering officer, who checked and double-checked his figures, but could not get the fuel to stretch as far as Norway. He thought that we might just about reach land up there if we did not deviate too much —so it was vital that our navigation was going to take us along the shortest practical route. Whichever way we went, we couldn't avoid the Atlantic—the option of going through the Strait of Dover or Pas de Calais was, of course, not open to us.

'Even at this comparatively mild time of year the swell heaved the boat considerably before dropping it into troughs. This was hardly upsetting for seasoned sailors, but some of the passengers had not even been on a pleasure cruise around Germany's bigger lakes, so they suffered considerably and added an even more foul odour to the already unbearable atmosphere.

'The boat was so exceedingly heavy with additional bodies and cargo that depth keeping was likely to become critical, especially if we came under attack and had to cope with machinery failure. Following

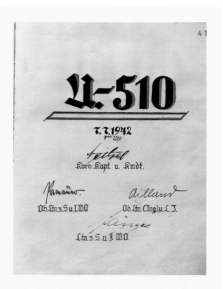

U510

U510 really needs to be included in this book because of the sheer audacity of the men who manned her. Fregkpt Karl Neitzel commanded the boat from 25 November 1941 until he put into Lorient on 16 April 1943, conveniently missing out on the carnage of Black May. Up till then he had attacked and at least damaged 12 ships and had been wearing a Knight's Cross around his neck for one month. What was to follow under Kptlt Alfred Eick, also a Knight of the Iron Cross, is even more remarkable. Although an ordinary ocean-going boat of Type IXC without additional fuel tanks, the men left on 3 November 1943 for a voyage to Penang, where they arrived on 5 April the following year. They then sailed on to Singapore and Kobe in Japan before starting a homeward run. A shortage of fuel made it impossible to reach Norway, so Eick took his boat into the besieged St Nazaire on 23 April 1945, just a couple weeks before the base surrendered to the French at the end of the war. It is a good indication of German workmanship that the boat was then taken over by the French Navy to be commissioned a second time with the new name of *Bouan*.

WP=10 + 3 transit patrols, S=--, K=--

some muttering, Pfeffer agreed that at least a couple of anti-convoy torpedoes should be jettisoned after their detonators had been removed. This reduced weight and made more room for aching bodies, but still did not allow them to stretch out. The majority were sitting, living and sleeping on metal floor plates, not an ideal way of travelling.

'The best piece of news came at lunchtime on 24 August 1944, when the Obersteuermann [navigator], Hugo Niepagenkemper, disclosed that we had covered 83 nautical miles during the last 24 hours. That was the most that we managed so far and brought a cheer throughout the cramped confines. Following this, we drifted back into a monotonous routine until five minutes before three in the morning of the following day, when alarm bells rang. The schnorkel head was quickly lowered before the boat dropped out of reach of the waves to settle in the depths. This time it levelled out, but didn't remain where it should. Instead, it kept sinking very slowly. Probably momentarily disorientated, the engineering officer, Oblt zur See (Ing) Josef Stürzinger, wondered whether there was a fault with the instruments, but all our depth gauges were indicating the same. Therefore, he increased speed so that the hydroplanes could make more impact, but even this hardly helped and we descended deeper. Of course, the majority of people were hardly aware of what was happening, but manning the depth-keeping control was unsettling and the commander sounded more than worried. Without consulting the engineering officer, he ordered, "Blow the tanks." These words had hardly left his mouth when the petty officer responsible for the control room announced that one of the diving valves had not been shut. The tanks were quickly pumped out and to everybody's relief, the boat responded.

'To make this potential disaster considerably worse, the boat had dived as a result of the first officer on periscope duty pressing the alarm bells. Consequently, everything happened rather quickly and a good amount of exhaust fumes vented into the boat, adding a choking pain to everybody's troubles. There was another problem. Somehow the radio did not work the way it should and although transmissions seemed to flow out, there was usually no reply, making us wonder whether the world had been closed down or whether we were not being heard. There were plenty of destroyers chasing about, so it looked as if the war was still going strong. Whether we had a radio or not hardly mattered, but a few days later the schnorkel started playing up and that was far more serious. On 29 August the damn air mast could not be raised at all. Each time it was elevated and locked into its bracket by the top of the conning tower,

water poured down by the bucket full. This was expelled again with the ballast pumps, but made it impossible to start the diesels for charging the batteries.

'Pfeffer stood perplexed for some time, watching the sequence over and over again, wondering what the men were doing wrong, when it occurred to everybody that it could not be the operators' fault. There had to be some other mechanical problem and the only way to find the gremlin was to surface. The boat was now dangerously near Ireland, making such an undertaking risky. Preparations were quick. I was one of the first lookouts on the conning tower. We were followed by the guncrews, and then the chief engineer and a petty officer examined the offending machinery. This time it was not their apparently long-winded investigation but the squeaking from the radar detector which gave everybody the jitters. Pfeffer almost lost his marbles, raised his voice and told the radio room to stop it screaming like an badly tuned radio or switch the blasted machine off. Luckily it did not come to an alarm dive. I didn't fancy our chances with so many men on the upper deck. This was the first time in a week that we had been on the surface and gave us the opportunity to empty our garbage containers. A good proportion of the fresh vegetable waste had started adding a disgustingly putrid smell to the interior.

'Some eight hours later, after we had been down again for a long time, came a most unusual call through the loudspeaker system, "Mechanikergefreiter Walter Heise report immediately to the commander." There was no response. He was one of the crew for the 37mm anti-aircraft gun on the lower platform and it looked as if he either didn't hear the order to dive or someone else reported to be the last man in. Whatever, there was no point in going back for the poor fellow. It would be another eight hours before we reached the spot and it would be dark when we got there. Even if he did survive until daylight the following day, it would be unlikely that we would find him in the vastness of the turbulent ocean.'

This loss was by no means an isolated case. At the back of U177's log is a comment by Konteradmiral Eberhard Godt (Chief of the Operations Department) saying:

'H. [not mentioned in the original log, this was Bootsmaat Erwin Henning] fell overboard without being noticed at a time when the boat was in utmost danger of being drowned by heavy waves. The commander and the crew concentrated on maintaining control of the boat. This was made more difficult by a jammed valve. Both the appalling weather and visibility deteriorated dramatically until the discovery that H. was missing and the long

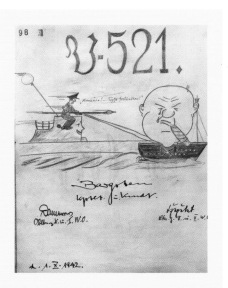

U521

The order shouted by Kptlt Klaus Bargsten on the bridge is, 'Galley! Hold on to the cooking pots.' He took U521 into Canadian waters and then into the central Atlantic and it was not long before he was awarded the Knight's Cross. He already had a large number of sinkings to his credit, having served as first watch officer of U99 under Otto Kretschmer, the highest scoring ace of World War II. The first watch officer usually aimed and shot torpedoes on the surface, so Bargsten made a significant contribution to Kretschmer's successful team. Like his old boss, Bargsten survived the sinking of his boat, yet he was shattered to discover that he was the only person to have got off before it was sunk some 360km east of Cape Hatteras in the United States. Exactly what happened is not clear, but it would seem that U521 was blown to the surface so severely damaged that Bargsten gave the order to abandon ship. Some sources suggest that the men went down while inside their boat while others suggest that they were shot while trying to escape from the sinking wreck.

WP=3, S=1, K=51

Above and Below left: Bringing supplies aboard U177 from Charlotte Schliemann (see page 102).

time made it pointless in turning round to attempt to find him.'

Heinz Fritsch again:

'There was another problem with U548 turning round. The schnorkel was still not functioning, meaning the boat had to surface once more, but this time with only first watch officer and the Obermaschinist on the top of the conning tower. Both men were told to shut the hatch. The plan was to dive as soon as the radar detector squeaked at the right volume and then come back to pick up the men. It was a drastic decision, but essential if we were going to survive. Working up in relatively mild weather, but in total darkness, could not have been easy and it didn't do much good. It didn't prevent water pouring down the schnorkel. Later it was discovered that the mechanism for operating some of the valves no longer functioned. It had been worn out. Therefore there was no choice other than to charge batteries on the surface and hope for the best.

'It seemed strange. We had now been at sea for 23 days. That's more than three weeks, and the majority of people just lurked silently in the small space they had made for themselves. There was hardly any conversation. Only the occasional news headlines from one of the working receivers were typed out and passed around. These made depressing reading, although the majority of lamps were switched off to conserve the batteries, making reading in the dark rather difficult. The Allies had taken Paris and were poised to march into Brussels. We got out of Lorient just in time. France was lost and the east wasn't any better. The Red Army was closing in on the Reich. It was best not to think or talk about it. On top of this, there was a desperate attempt to kill Hitler in his headquarters, but the assassination misfired and the perpetrators have been caught.

'God knows how many times we were driven into the cellar. Even with the logbook at hand it is difficult to count the attacks. There were so many that Pfeffer gave up recording them individually. The pains of everyday life merged from one monotony into another, actions were automatic and one didn't complain. The next major shock came shortly after midnight of 9 September. We had just surfaced. The diesel engines burst into life and then, with a loud muffled bang, one of them stopped and then there was silence. The commander had to ask what happened, but it took a while before a report was forthcoming. The inside of the diesel compartment was not too comfortable and one needed to be rather technical to understand the damage, but it added up to having to run on one engine, meaning we had to remain on the surface for twice as long. The engineers battled for the best part of 24 hours before the problem

was rectified and they dared to re-start the offending engine.

'Although we could receive radio signals, sending them still presented a number of problems. But that hardly mattered. We were on our own without support. It was up to us to reach Norway or perish. The opposition must have known where we were by now. We had been chased into the cellar too often and anyone with any common sense could have plotted our course from the sighting reports. On the other hand, the English might be resting on their laurels, thinking that we were already dead. For most of the time we managed no more than 50 miles per day— and god knows how many thousands of miles it was from France to Norway. I didn't dare look at the chart: seeing the long distance still to go would have been too demoralising. It was best to take every duty as it came and before dropping into bed, pray that we would still be alive for the next turn.

'Things started getting even more drastic on 24 September, when there was such constant air cover that we had to remain submerged for two days. God knows what went through the minds of the passengers. Food was bloody lousy by now and the air was more than foul, so perhaps they were more anaesthetised than the rest of us. There were a number of cases of people dropping into unconsciousness and Pfeffer gave a strict orders that we should neither move nor make a noise. I was sitting painfully at the hydroplanes when the old man crawled into the central control room. The effort had virtually been too much and he had to take several deep breaths before picking up the microphone. Gasping for air,

he said, "Now listen men. You are going to get a good meal and then everybody will put on their escape apparatus and get ready to evacuate the boat. Only men necessary to set scuttling charges will to remain behind. End of message." For a while he stood there panting heavily. Even those few words were hard going with so little air left.

'Commander, first officer and lookouts were ready for the bridge. Everybody realised when the hatch was opened because the reduction in pressure was noticeable in the ears. But then, instead of staring death in the face, both sky and sea were clear. Only gently rolling empty waves. Nothing else. Whatever had kept us down for so long had gone home. Consequently there was an immediate change in plans. Diesels were started and instantly driven to fast speed. It wasn't long before another ship appeared in front of us. The batteries were more exhausted than the men, meaning there was no way we could dive and it was a case of preparing the interior for destruction. Then, at that crucial moment of doom, the ship flashed a German recognition signal. It

seemed impossible. I couldn't believe it. It had to be a dream.

'It was at 23:00 hours on 25 September 1944 that the order, "Prepare upper deck for making fast," was given. Twenty minutes later we tied up behind U483 in Bergen. We had been at sea for an unexpected 46 days and nights, covered a total of 2,716 nautical miles or 5,030km and only 907 of those miles were on the surface. For the rest of the voyage the boat had been submerged. The ordeal was over. We were still alive.'

The European coastal waters, especially the Bay of Biscay, saw considerable carnage during the summer of 1944 with U-boats coming off exceedingly badly. A few more boats managed to get out of the beleaguered French ports to reach Norway or Germany, but the majority that attempted a breakout did not get very far. The departures of boats which were lost, in chronological order, were listed by Heinz Fritsch as shown below—not many reached safe waters.

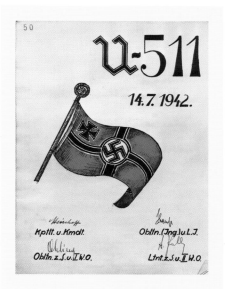

U511

Kptlt Friedrich Steinhoff, whose signature appears on this page of the visitors' book, later took command of *U873*, which he surrendered in America at the end of the war. Having given themselves up, according to orders from the U-boat Command, the men were so badly treated that Steinhoff committed suicide to escape the pain. He had a brother working at the German rocket research station at Peenemünde and at one stage helped him with the launching of rockets from the submerged *U511*. The last patrol took the *U511*, under Kptlt Fritz Schneewind, to Penang where it was handed over to the Japanese Navy to become *RO-500*. The German crew remained in the Far East as replacements for men from other boats which started arriving in Japanese occupied territory towards the end of the war.

WP=4, S=--, K=--

July 1944

22	St Nazaire	U667	OL Karl-Heinz Lange, mined on the way into La Pallice with 45 lives.
26	Brest	U984	OL Heinz Sieder, lost with 45 lives.
26	Boulogne	U671	KL Wolfgang Hegewald, lost en-route to Lorient with 47 lives.

August 1944

2	Brest	U413	OL Dietrich Sachse, sunk in the Channel with 45 lives.
3	Le Havre	U741	OL Gerhard Palmgren, sunk in the Channel with 48 lives.
5	Lorient	U736	OL Reinhard Reff, sunk with 28 lives.
7	Lorient	U608	OL Wolfgang Reisener, sunk by a Liberator.*
7	Lorient	U981	OL Günther Keller, lost en-route to La Pallice with a loss of 12 lives.
9	St Nazaire	U385	KL Hans-Guido Valentiner lost with one life.
10	Lorient	U270	OL Heinrich Schreiber.**
11	Brest	U618	OL Erich Faust, lost en-route to La Pallice with 61 lives.
13	Brest	U621	OL Hermann Stuckmann, lost en-route to La Pallice with 56 lives.
14	Horten	U484	KK Wolf-Axel Schaefer, sunk near the Hebrides with 52 lives.
16	Lorient	U107	KL Volker Simmermacher, lost en-route to La Pallice with 59 lives.
21	Bergen	U743	OL Helmut Kandzior, lost near Ireland, cause unknown, with 50 lives.
22	Lorient	U445	OL Rupprecht Fischler, Graf von Treuberg.***
22	Bordeaux	U180	OL Rolf Riesen, mined with a loss of 56 lives.
22	Kristiansand	U925	OL Helmuth Knocke, lost with 51 lives.

September 1944

8	Trondheim	U865	OL Dietrich Stellmacher, lost to an unknown cause with 59 lives.
12	Kristiansand	U867	Kpt zur See Arved von Mühlendahl, sunk with 60 lives.

The following boats were so badly damaged that they had to be scuttled: *U123* and *U129* in Lorient, *U178* and *U188* in Bordeaux and *U766* in La Pallice.

*   The entire crew of 51 was saved by the sloop HMS *Wren*.
**   *U270* left with 81 people on board and 71 of these were saved when this standard Type VIIC was sunk.
*** Lost en route to Norway with 53 lives. Before this *U445* had left Brest on 12 August 1944 for an evacuation to Lorient.

Top left: *U548* in Holefjord (Norway) where the crew recovered from their incredible ordeal of having escaped from France. This was an ocean-going boat of Type IXC/40.

Above left: Oblt.z.S. Horst Günther in January 1945 after he had become First Watch Officer of U3022, a new, large electro-boat of Type XXI, which was due to have replaced Type VII and IX in the Atlantic.

Bases

Following the end of World War I, the Allies made sure that German naval bases were wrecked beyond use by removing the majority of modern installations. At the same time, the size of the armed forces was drastically reduced so that the navy consisted of no more than 15,000 men. This meant that there was an abundance of empty buildings for the small fledgling Reichsmarine and consequently there was ample accommodation.

During those depressing years immediately after World War I, the agricultural eastern provinces suffered considerably worse than those of the west, and an urgent investment of industrial muscle was going to be required to solve the massive unemployment problem there. However, the navy was not terribly keen on contributing towards the development of port facilities in the east because a large part of that area had been taken away from Germany by the Allies, to form part of the new Polish Republic. The reconstituted country stretched as far as the Baltic shores, dividing Germany into two separate zones. Crossing this so-called Polish corridor was felt to be a humiliating nightmare for civilians and virtually impossible for the military. German passenger trains, for example, had to be locked and often it was also necessary for the curtains to be closed so that the occupants should not catch glimpses of the surrounding countryside. On top of this, Polish authorities made it difficult to maintain schedules, often creating long delays for a multitude of petty reasons. With such a hostile hold on the territory, it was thought that military establishments in East Prussia would be too vulnerable to being isolated by foreign authorities.

This changed as soon as World War II started and the German military machine was quick in spreading into the eastern regions. The main reason for this enthusiasm was that the area was well beyond reach of French and British aircraft, making places there ideal training centres. This meant that the majority of operational headquarters remained in Berlin, Kiel or Wilhelmshaven and some other western towns, while the rapidly increasing number of support services took advantage of the comparative safety provided by the eastern provinces. The vast majority of command

centres, with the exception of the Supreme Naval Command in Berlin, were established as mobile units, making it relatively easy to spread into available space, wherever it happened to be. By spring 1940, when Germany had occupied Holland, Belgium and parts of France, training had expanded on such a massive scale that the few eastern establishments could no longer cope, and many educational units were set up on foreign soil. The majority of these locations were chosen because they provided the necessary accommodation in the form of military barracks, disused factories or other large buildings, and a good number were in fairly inaccessible backwaters.

Obviously, strategic requirements played a significantly large role in the building-up of operational bases in occupied countries. Since many of these were within reach of the Royal Air Force, U-boat harbours had to be placed under concrete by building what has been claimed to be the biggest bunkers ever. However, this is not true because a number of civilian shelters in Germany were even more impressive than many of the huge submarine pens.

Very quickly there developed two contrasting types of U-boat base. On the one hand there were the major centres, providing a wealth of services including dry docks and heavy repair facilities, and on the other were small ports where only fuel, water and provisions could be topped up to provide a few extra days at sea. One such place was Kristiansand on the southern tip

Above: The U-boat tender *Weichsel*, named after the river flowing through Danzig in East Prussia. Unlike British depot ships, these acted more as floating headquarters and accommodation ships rather than workshops.

of Norway. Many U-boats called on these smaller places for only very brief periods, often so short that there was not even time to allow men a run ashore.

Shortly after the beginning of the war, the majority of operational U-boats at sea were controlled from land-based command centres, while those in ports were looked after by flotilla staff. Additional services, such communications, were usually provided by other autonomous offices. 'Command centres' is in the plural because some boats in the Arctic, all boats in the Mediterranean, those in the Black Sea and the wolfpacks of the Atlantic were controlled by different authorities. Flotilla commanders did not have operational control of U-boats, except occasionally in their immediate coastal areas. As far as actions at sea were concerned, it hardly mattered to which flotilla a boat belonged because they were all controlled by the same operations room on land and mingled with submarines from any flotilla, that happened to be in the same area. Some boats, especially those with experienced commanders on long voyages, were given

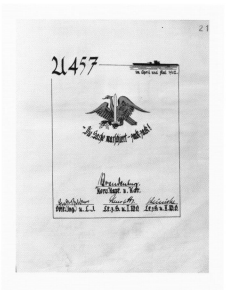

U457

U457 was Korvkpt Karl Brandenburg's one and only command. He took the boat on six operational patrols into Arctic seas to sink three ships in those cold and desolate waters, and even had a go at hunting the famous Convoy PQ17. All 45 men on board were killed by depth charges from the destroyer HMS *Impulsive* on 16 September 1942 to the west of Novaya Zemlya. Brandenburg was quite old for the U-boat arm, having been born on 25 July 1906. He was a young lad at school when World War I ended and he joined the small Reichsmarine during a turbulent period in 1924. Towards the beginning of World War II he served with a land-based naval artillery unit before going on for submarine training.

WP=6(?), S=0, K=45

Above left: Flotilla Weddigen before the war with (from left to right) *U17*, *U15*, *U13*. This type of mooring was common during the early years and later in areas which could not be reached by enemy aircraft. Such a bunch of boats presented too big a target for bombers and making fast side by side was prohibited once the war started. The boats are flying naval war flags on the stern and on the bows the national-cum-mercantile flag—similar to the Reich service flag, but with an eagle and swastika in the top left-hand corner.

Below left: Small training boats lying next to a depot ship in the Baltic, where there is no tide and little danger from enemy aircraft.

considerable autonomy to do what they pleased within the restrictions of their operations orders, while others had virtually every move directed by the operations room. This went as far as the Commander-in-Chief, Admiral Karl Dönitz, reminding his men that the coming of a new moon period was going to mean there would be a few exceptionally dark nights ideally suitable for attacking.

The main U-boat bases had either one or two resident flotillas and the commanders of these were responsible for providing everything needed by crews while in port, as well as provisioning and repairing boats for their next voyage. These leaders were experienced ex-U-boat commanders.

In port it was general practice to give men as much time off as possible, but some of the crew usually remained with the boat in a supervisory nature. Virtually everything was removed from the interior for cleaning or locked away to assure that foreign workers could not gain access to vital secrets. Once this had been done, the majority of men worked office hours, giving them the chance to seek out some enjoyment during the evenings and only about three or four remained on guard duty.

As far as possible, men were accommodated in barracks or in other land-based accommodation. Officers usually lived in hotels or similar establishments, where civilian staff cleaned their quarters. Other ranks were more often allocated plainer rooms where they had to do their own cleaning. On the one hand, men were free go and come as they pleased, with as few restrictions as possible, but on the other it was necessary to maintain quite a strict hold on their behaviour and there were stringent rules for conduct on land. For example: female visitors were not allowed in bedrooms, sailors were not allowed in buildings occupied by civilians, drinking was only permitted in the bars and strictly prohibited in corridors and bedrooms. Married men were allowed unprotected sexual intercourse with their wives, but condoms had to be worn for sexual contact with any other person. There appear to be no hard and fast rules about how these small pieces of essential gear were issued, but it seems likely that there were times when men had to buy their own, while on other occasions they were available free from the quartermaster's stores. Whatever, they were readily available. A large number of vending

U443

'Whoever is gripped by the griffin will be cracked …' seems to have come true. *U443* sunk four ships, including a corvette during three patrols under Oblt zur See Konstantin von Puttkamer, but this spell of good luck didn't last. Everybody on board was killed when the boat was depth-charged by RN frigates *Bicester*, *Lamerton* and *Wheatland* on 23 February 1943, one week after having left the home port of La Spezia in the Mediterranean. There was one more officer in the navy with this unusual surname: Karl-Jesko von Puttkamer was Hitler's naval adjutant.

WP=3, S=0, K=48

Above left: On the right the Tirpitz Pier, Kiel, with a number of small training boats.

Far left: The main entrance to the naval base at Wilhelmshaven photographed on 17 July 1936.

Left: The Penfeld River in Brest with high level swing bridge for public traffic and floating pontoon bridge for naval access. This was the hub of the naval base before the large U-boat bunker was built. The area has been modernised and rebuilt but much of it is still the same as it was in 1944, although the high level, rotating bridge has been replaced by a new, lifting structure.

Left: The garden side of a building used for accommodating U-boat men in Lorient (France).

Right: For much of the time U-boat men had to make do with all-male company, but occasionally there were opportunities for socialising with female workers. This picture was taken inside an underground bunker during a party with female aircraft watchers— the equivalent of the British Observer Corps, who monitored enemy aircraft near the bases.

machines were placed in public lavatories, stations, hotels and other places likely to be frequented by soldiers.

The reason for wearing condoms was not to avoid unwanted pregnancies, but to prevent the spreading of sexually transmitted diseases. The fear of putting entire boats out of action by such infections was uppermost in the minds of administrators and therefore an adequate supply was usually provided. There is rather a bitter story of German troops being cut off in the wastes of Russia without supplies for a considerable period. When food and ammunition were finally flown in to the already starving and freezing garrison, the supplies included large boxes of condoms, despite there being no females within hundreds of kilometres. To have sex without a condom was a punishable offence and anyone indulging in such practice was tried by court martial. A number of charge sheets, with details of such proceedings, are still stored in the U-Boot-Archiv and make fascinating reading. One wonders how these offences were discovered in the first place. It must have been as a result of bragging by the culprit.

A good proportion of sailors in the naval bases were away from home for the first time. Therefore, it was not unexpected that they should behave like a bunch of liberated students. Their high spirits often overflowed with powerful, pent-up emotions and the feeling of being 'free' in port was similar to activating a detonator on a bomb. It must also be remembered that some of these youngsters came into port after having cheated an excruciatingly painful death on more than one occasion and they knew that they might not come back from the next trip. Therefore they lived life to the full, taking advantage of everything on offer. Kpt zur See Otto Köhler of *U377* and Kpt zur See 'Ajax' Bleichrodt of *U48*, *U67* and *U109* both said that the tenseness of action at sea kept their

minds from wandering, but once in port it was a case of getting drunk to prevent them from considering the more unpleasant aspects of what they were doing. The authorities didn't seem to mind drunk sailors, as long as they were not disorderly. At the end of the war, Geoff Henderson, a South African pilot serving with the Royal Air Force, was most impressed to discover that the messes in their occupied bases had special, high level sinks to be sick into.

As far as people living in the bases were concerned, the biggest problem was that the majority of U-boat men had hardly any experience with alcohol or with girls. Indeed the vast proportion did not receive sex education at school. This subject was hardly discussed during those times and most U-boat men had very little knowledge of the opposite sex. It has been difficult to gain an insight from the view of the many prostitutes who plied their trade among these inexperienced youngsters, but Margaret Wiese, a German secretary in the

Naval Arsenal in Brest, wrote to her mother:

'... *the behaviour of German U-boat men is appalling and they were best avoided, especially at night, when it is impossible to be out alone. French men hardly ever trouble us, but the culprits are always German U-boat crews running amok. They are often incapable of even standing up on their own and frequently use the stairwell leading to flats occupied by female workers as a lavatory. The sad point about this disgusting behaviour is that very little can be done about it. Complaining means filling in forms and writing out the details, which is so complicated that it is hardly worth the effort. To make matters worse, by the time the individuals are identified, they have gone back to sea again and the matter is forgotten.'*

Gaining sexual contact with girls was a good deal easier than marrying them, although the navy put very few obstacles in

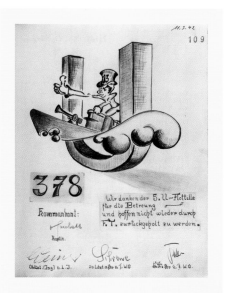

U378

The inscription, 'We thank the 5th Flotilla for their care and hope that we are not recalled again by RT', suggests that *U378* under Kptlt Alfred Hoschatt got off to a frustrating start. Even once under way, there seems to have been some trouble because the boat stopped at Heligoland for three days in March 1942 before heading north to the Kola Inlet. A number of other boats followed the same routine at about the same time, suggesting that mines along the way ahead, rather than mechanical breakdown, were the problem. Although *U378* sailed on a number of war patrols, it sank only one ship. Hoschatt survived the war and was one of the officers responsible for helping Günter Hessler write an interesting three-volume work on the Battle of the Atlantic, which has now been published by HMSO.

WP=8, S=0, K=48

way and tended to encourage the formation of families. There were even medals for mothers who produced an abundance of children. However, permission had to be obtained first from naval authorities by filling out the appropriate form. There was at least one case of a young girl marrying the corpse of a U-boat commander. The two were officially engaged and enjoyed a few days of leave together in the privacy of a bed. When she discovered that she was pregnant, he was already classed as missing and a few days later his corpse was washed up on a French beach. Wanting her child to have the same name as the father, she was offered the opportunity of a posthumous marriage. Sadly, her only son committed suicide around the time he was doing his university entrance examinations and it looks highly likely that the mother has since died as well. However, in case she is still alive, it will be best to maintain her anonymity here.

For most of the time, Margaret Wiese could only communicate superficially with her mother by writing letters. International telephone connections did exist, but these were so complicated that they were hardly used by ordinary people. In any case, very few people had telephones during those times. On 4 April 1943 she started a long typewritten letter because one of her colleagues was going to deliver it personally while home on leave. Therefore, since this was definitely going to miss a censor, she felt that she could describe some things she could not mention in an ordinary letter. Much of her news was of a private nature about her poor health, but there are some fascinating snippets about life in a main U-boat base and the following excerpts might be of general interest:

'I came home feeling pretty bad and collapsed into bed without undressing. Then, after a couple of hours, I took my clothes off. It was a dark, overcast day with low cloud, so I wasn't scared about an imminent air raid and did not have to sleep fully clothed ... The people below me came home with visitors and turned the radio very loud. Most inconsiderate ... The trouble with being ill is that one is immediately suspected of trying to dodge work and one must bear in mind that all the doctors here have come from a male-orientated, military background. They cannot imagine the problems encountered by women. Since my periods have been so especially bad, I was accused of having had a self-made abortion and I had to have exceedingly stern words with the doctor to make it clear that this was not the case. It would seem that the doctors cannot think of anything else ... My period bleeding has been especially bad, which means that I spoilt a number of my best clothes and cannot get them clean here. There is no way that I can lay the clothes out on the lawn to bleach. You must get fed up with me sending you parcels with dirty clothes to wash. But there is no way that I can get them clean here. The facilities are just not to hand ... It was Saturday lunch time, when I was feeling especially lousy that I went to bed. I was in deep sleep when the air raid sirens howled away. Oh, it is so awful to be dragged in such a crude manner out of deep sleep. And then my clothes and shoes were not lying ready the way I usually arrange them. Consequently it took a while to get dressed and leave the flat. Despite feeling so awful, I dragged myself down to the air raid shelter. Once outside, I noticed the birds in the convent garden opposite and the warm sun beating down from a blue sky. Among all this I am terrified of dying a horrible death and chase along as fast as my feet can carry me. I wonder whether there will ever again be a life without air raids and without the fear of constant death. I wonder what life would be like if it were not for this awful war. Undressing to go to bed seems to be a thing

Above left: Accommodation in France. The radio was not official naval issue, but such sets were hired out by local entrepreneurs, who found an avid acceptance for their services. Such radios were often left on all night so that the men would be woken by the beginning of transmissions at 05:00 or 06:00 in the morning. The noise of a humming radio hardly troubled U-boat men, who were used to sleeping with high levels of engine noise.

of the past. We always sleep fully clothed so that we can get away quickly and a number of people carry heavy bags with their vital belongings ... Then there was a case of one of our workers who stole some cable. He was caught very quickly and taken to the cells. At that moment his place of work received a direct hit and his mates were killed outright, while this guilty person survived. Somehow life is not fair... Incidentally things have become so chaotic here with a good number of unidentified corpses that everybody, including us civilian workers, has to wear metal identification tags around the neck, the same as the military. It makes it easier to deal with corpses.

'A few days ago I came from doing some shopping after work and had just got my coat and shoes off when the air raid sirens howled... This time I bought 2kg of potatoes, 1kg of carrots, a bundle of leeks, a cauliflower, a tin of peas and 12 eggs which came to 148 Francs. This is equal to RM 7.40 [RM=Reichsmark]. So you see money disappears very quickly. I bought a large piece of stewing meat for RM12, but that was really too much for one so I wanted to share it with Lischen, but she said that it was too expensive ... The 2nd Depot is burning fiercely and many of the French workers have been sent home because there is nothing for them to do. I was rather concerned about Carsten, who lives close by. Much of the dock yard looks pretty bad with many bombed out buildings ... I had hardly reached the office when there was another one of those dreadful alarms. This time I hurried to the shelter inside the cliffs. Most of us can get there within five minutes or so, but it is always terribly crowded with everybody pushing and shoving around ... When we got out we found that the emergency accommodation for the bombed-out workers has been hit as well and those people living there have now lost everything in a mass of flames. Good job that most of the people had left it in time before it was hit.'

It may be interesting to add that the British public was told in September 1944 that the damage in Brest could not have been caused by the Allied bombing offensive, but was the result of the Germans spraying houses with petrol and then setting them alight.

'I met Carsten. He was carrying a suitcase and is all right ... The bomb hits are creeping ever closer to the office where I work and it can't be long before they get us as well. I wonder whether this terror will ever stop again and whether there will ever be a time when we can live without the fear of death ... With things getting so bad, I asked whether it might be possible to deposit a suitcase with belongings inside the bunker. After all, there appears to be plenty of space and that would at least give

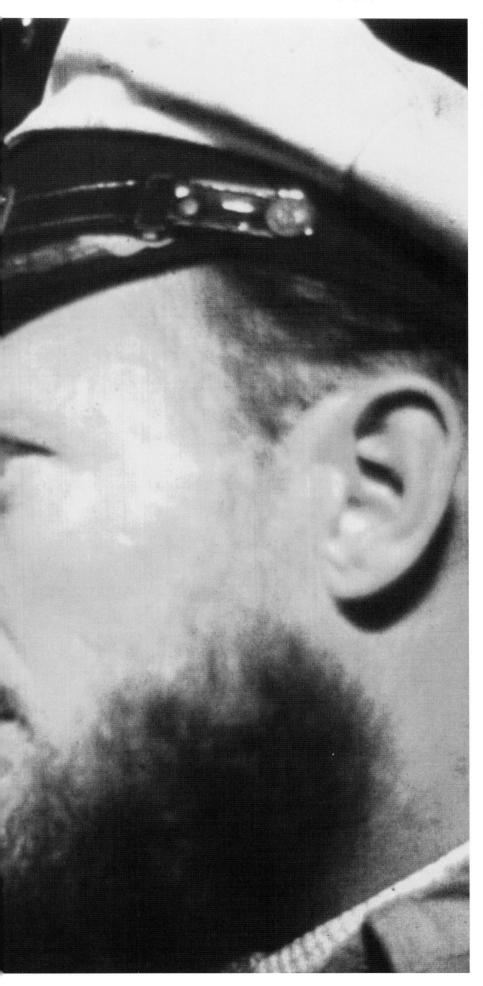

U173

The key, which also featured as a fully blown emblem on the conning tower, is the main part of Bremen's coat of arms. The first commander, Fregkpt Heinz-Ehler Beucke, chose it because it had not featured on any boat and he wanted to acknowledge the efforts put in by the people of the city where it was built. *U173* left for two operational tours, each under a different commander. Beucke survived the war to become a prisoner, but his successor, Oblt zur See Hans-Adolf Schweichel, went down with his 56 men when the boat was depth-charged by the US destroyers *Woolsey*, *Swanson* and *Quick* on 16 November 1942. During its short life *U173* sank one ship and damaged three others. Not a great deal of return for the fantastic effort put into its creation, but better than the vast majority that never got within shooting distance of the enemy.

WP=2, S=0, K 57

Left: Robert Gysae at the periscope shortly after his promotion to Korvettenkapitän. It looks very much as if this is the attack periscope, which usually had only one eyepiece, while the much bigger navigation or sky periscope had two eyepieces.

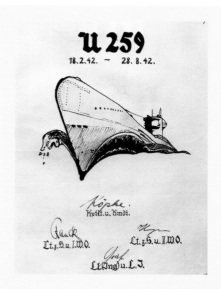

U259

Above: Men of *U251* being greeted back in port while the commander, Heinrich or 'Tüte' Timm, with the white cap, looks on.

Left: *U1007* under Kptlt Hans Hornkohl leaving the accommodation ship *Albatross* in Kiel towards the end of May 1944.

me the peace if mind that I have a few basic essentials if we are bombed. But the answer was a definite no … Much of the city is like a ghost town. Every third house is derelict. It has either been bombed or, if it is still standing, the occupants have left. Either they have fled or they are already dead … it is Saturday again. Very overcast with low clouds, but that doesn't mean air raid free any more. Yesterday was similar and we had three alarms during the day. The 2nd Depot has been burning for some time, but it has now been extinguished because there is nothing left to burn. All that is left is the hollow stonework. It appears that the fire there could not be put out during the early stages because there was no water. Then, when it was flowing again they found the hoses so blocked with tools and rags that the fire engines would not work. It is dreadful. The majority of people there have nothing other than the dirty work clothes which they were wearing before the raid started … I really need a new coat, but there seems to be no point in buying one. They are expensive, poor quality and once you have worn them three times inside the rock bunker you find that your clothes are so dirty that they can only be worn in the dark. Mrs Koch has had the skin on her arm scraped off by being dragged along the rough rocky walls. We also heard that one woman was recently trampled to death in the bunker.

'Friday, 16 April 1943. It is half past three in the afternoon. We have endured another heavy air attack. We had just reached the staircase on our way to lunch when it started with the sirens wailing. This time we had to cross what looked like a building site to get to a shelter inside the cliffs, where the majority of people from the dock quarter go. It is dreadful there. You have to run through mud and over stones and railway tracks. Dirty water is continuously dripping down from the rocks to make awful spots on your clothes. Luckily I was wearing my blue jacket which did not show the mess so much, but my shoes and stockings look dreadful. To make matters even worse, they had been blasting inside the tunnel, leaving the air filled with a dreadful smell of gunpowder. This stench, together with dirty people, was quite horrible. The bomb blasts created terrific shock waves throughout the rocky tunnels so that people had to hold on to the railway trucks or wet rock walls to prevent themselves being blown over. It seems that the doors were not working properly and could not be shut completely. Then, suddenly and without warning the lights went out. There is a narrow gauge railway inside for the builders and this made moving about quite difficult. It was bearable where we were, but it must have been pretty bad further in, where the air was even worse. There were fumes coming in from outside in addition to the painful dust. People couldn't cope and amidst this darkness people were being carried out. We were in there for one and a half hours. In the end we could hardly stand any longer. When we did get outside we found a clear blue sky with sun shining as if nothing had happened. The fresh air was good, but our nostrils were blocked with a black soot-like material. The clearness didn't last long.

U259 was commissioned by Kptlt Klaus Köpke on 18 February 1942 and left Kiel on 29 August to travel to La Pallice via the North Atlantic. From there it was ordered into the Mediterranean. Although having negotiated the narrow Strait of Gibraltar without too much trouble, *U259* ran into the Allied landings of North Africa, and was spotted on the surface by a Hudson aircraft. The lookouts on the conning tower did not see their attacker until it was too late to dive. Instead of going down, Köpke ordered full speed to fight it out on the surface, but an accurate straddle of depth charges sank the boat and damaged the aircraft piloted by Flying Officer M. A. Ensor from No 500 Squadron, RAF, which ditched in the sea shortly before reaching Algiers, a few miles to the south.

WP=2, S=0, K=48

Left: A large army of administrators and workers had to make a considerable effort for everything to run smoothly once a boat came into port. Accommodation had to be provided, the men's personal belongings brought out of store from their last port of call and mail organised. This shows post being distributed in St Nazaire to men of *U71*.

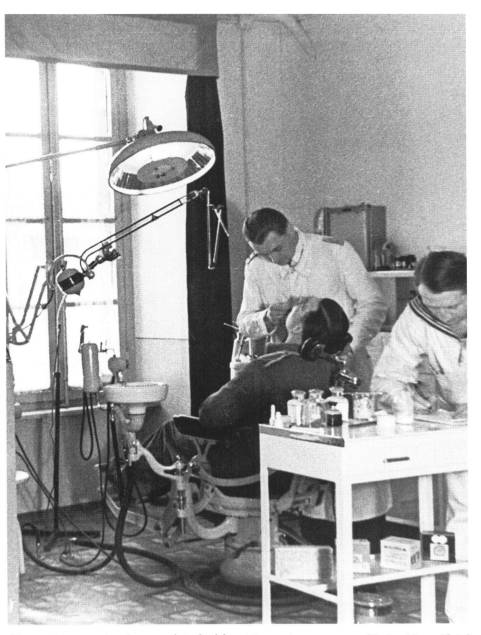

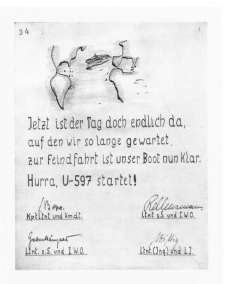

Jetzt ist der Tag doch endlich da,
auf den wir so lange gewartet,
zur Feindfahrt ist unser Boot nun klar.
Hurra, U-597 startet!

Kptlt und Kmdt.

Ltnt z.S. und I.W.O.

Ltnt. z.S. und I.W.O.

Ltnt.(Ing) und L.I.

U597

'At last the day has arrived for which we have been waiting for and now the boat is ready for a war patrol.' Kptlt Eberhard Bopst may have been keen to strike at the enemy, but it was not long before he met someone keener to kill him. It was during his second cruise into the North Atlantic, on 12 October 1942, that he was sighted near Rockall by a Liberator from No 120 Squadron, RAF, under Sqn Ldr T. M. Bulloch, who was the highest scoring U-boat hunter in the RAF. Catching U597 on the surface while it was in the process of diving, he straddled it with a number of such well-placed depth charges that the airmen saw the boat break up before taking its final plunge. There was no escape from such a deadly hit.

WP=2, S=0, K=49

Above: Ports tend to be associated with bars, alcohol and prostitutes, yet they also had more mundane functions, as evinced by this naval dentist's surgery.

Above left: U31 being loaded prior to leaving as a member of an international peacekeeping force off Spain during the civil war there. The red, white and black stripes of the old Weimar Republic on the conning tower served as identification. This shows just a fraction of stores which had to be taken on board through small hatches in the 'ceiling' and stowed inside an already cramped interior.

Below left: U143, a coastal boat of Type IID, passing the type of liner used for accommodation in the main naval bases. Since there were a large number of passenger ships unable to ply their trade at sea, they were used to ease the burden of housing in what often were quite small seaside towns.

The entire area was filled with artificial fog. No wonder. The sirens howled again suggesting that there were more aircraft on the way.'

It is rather interesting that this portrayal of fright was not shared by U-boat men, many of whom looked upon air raids as a means of livening up an otherwise boring period in dock. It was possible to watch the aircraft approach, release their bombs and then there was still time to get away from the entrances of the bunker. Once the first detonations started, the commotion didn't last terribly long and was felt to be nowhere near as bad as depth charge attacks on submarines.

Bibliography

Beaver, Paul: *U-boats in the Atlantic*; Patrick Stephens Ltd, Cambridge, 1979. An interesting collection of photographs from the Bundesarchiv, but with some questionable captions.

Brennecke, Jochen: *Jäger—Gejagte*; Koehlers Verlag, Jugendheim, 1956. One of the early classics with excellent descriptions of life aboard U-boats.

Brunswig, Hans: *Feuersturm über Hamburg*; Motorbuch Verlag, Stuttgart, 1992. An excellent book about the terrifying raids on Hamburg.

Brustat-Naval, Fritz: *Ali Cremer—U333*; Ullstein, Frankfurt am Main, 1982.

Brustat-Naval, Fritz:and Suhren, Teddy; *Nasses Eichenlaub*; Koehlers, Herford, 1983.

Buchheim, Lothar-Günther; *Ubootskrieg*; Piper, Munich, 1976. Contains a vast number of fascinating photographs taken by the author while serving as war correspondent.

Busch, Harald; *So war der Ubootskrieg*; Deutsche Heimat Verlag, Bielefeld, 1954. This early account by an ex-war-correspondent has become a classic on this subject.

Busch, Rainer and Röll, Hans-Joachim: *Der U-Boot-Krieg 1939 bis 1945. Vol 1, Die deutschen U-Boot-Kommandanten*; Koehler/Mittler, Hamburg, Berlin, Bonn 1996. Published in English by Greenhill as *U-boat Commanders*. Brief biographies produced from the records of the German U-boot-Archiv. Sadly the English edition has been published without the numerous corrections recorded by the Archiv.

Busch, Rainer and Röll, Hans-Joachim: *Der U-Boot-Krieg 1939-1945*; E.S. Mittler & Sohn, Hamburg, Berlin and Bonn 1999. German U-boat losses from September 1939 to May 1945 from the records of the U-Boot-Archiv.

Compton-Hall, Richard: *The Underwater War 1939-45*; Blandford Press, Poole, 1982. The author was the Director of the Royal Navy's Submarine Museum and this is by far the best book for describing life in submarines.

Cremer, Peter: *U-boat Commander*; The Bodley Head, London, 1982.

Deutscher Marinebund: *Ubootsmuseum U995*; Laboe.

Deutsches Marineinstitut: Marineschule Mürwik; E.S. Mittler & Sohn, Herford.

Dönitz, Karl: *Ten Years and Twenty Days*; Weidenfeld and Nicolson, London, 1959.

Dönitz, Karl: *Mein wechselvolles Leben*; Musterschmidt Verlag, Frankfurt, 1968.

Drummond, John D.: *H.M.U-boat*; W. H. Allen, London, 1958. The story of *U570* after its capture, when it was renamed HMS *Graph*.

Frank, Dr. Wolfgang: *Die Wölfe und der Admiral*; Gerhard Stalling Verlag, Oldenburg, 1953. Translated as *Sea Wolves – The Story of the German U-boat War*. Weidenfeld, London, 1955. An excellent classic written by a war correspondent who served aboard U-boats.

Gasaway, E. B.: *Grey Wolf, Grey Sea*; Arthur Barker, London, 1972. (The fascinating story of U124.)

Gellermann, Günther W.: *Der andere Auftrag*; Bernard & Graefe, Bonn 1997. Interesting and detailed accounts about agents landed on foreign shores.

Giese, Otto and Wise, Capt. James E.: *Shooting the War*; Naval Institute Press, Annapolis, 1994. A fascinating book. Giese ran the blockade aboard the merchant ship *Anneliese Essberger* and then joined the U-boat Arm to serve in the Arctic, Atlantic and Far East.

Gröner, Erich: *Die deutschen Kriegsschiffe 1815 – 1945*; J.F. Lehmanns, Munich, 1968. This is the standard book on the technical data of German warships. Much of the information is tabulated, making it relatively easy for non-German readers. However, the section dealing with U-boat losses contains a good proportion of questionable information.

Gröner, Erich: *Die Handelsflotten der Welt 1942*; J.F. Lehmanns, Munich, reprinted 1976. Includes details of ships sunk up to 1942. This valuable publication was originally a confidential document and contains a complete list of ships, in similar style to Lloyds Register. There is also a lengthy section with good line drawings.

Hadley, Michael L.: *U-boats against Canada*; McGill-Queen's University Press, Kingston and Montreal, 1985. An excellent book with detailed information about U-boats which approached the Canadian coast.

Hadley, Michael L.: *Count not the Dead*; McGill-Queen's University Press, Montreal, Kingston and London, 1995.

Hering, Robert: *Chronik der Crew 37A 1937 – 1987*; Selbstverlag, Gärtringen, 1987. An excellent account about officers who joined the navy in 1937.

Herzog, Bodo: *60 Jahre deutsche Uboote 1906-1966*; J.F. Lehmanns, Munich, 1968. A useful book with much tabular information.

Herzog, Bodo; *U-boats in Action*; Ian Allan, Shepperton and Podzun, Dorheim. A pictorial book with captions in English.

Hessler, Günter, Hoschatt, Alfred and others: *The U-boat War in the Atlantic*; HMSO, 1989.

Hirschfeld, Wolfgang: *Feindfahrten*; Neff, Vienna, 1982. The secret diary of a U-boat radio operator compiled in the radio rooms of operational submarines. A most invaluable insight into the war and probably one of the most significant accounts of the war at sea.

Hirschfeld, Wolfgang: *Das Letzte Boot – Atlantik Farewell*; Universitas, Munich, 1989. The last journey of *U234*, surrender in the United States and life as prisoner of war.

Hirschfeld, Wolfgang and Geoffrey Brooks; *Hirschfeld—The Story of a U-boat NCO 1940-46*; Leo Cooper, London, 1996. A fascinating English language edition of Hirschfeld's life in U-boats.

Hoffmann, Rudolf: *50 Jahre Olympia-Crew*; Selbstverlag, Hamburg 1986 and 1988. An excellent account about the men who joined the navy in 1936.

Högel, Georg: *Embleme Wappen Malings deutscher Uboote 1939--1945*; Koehlers, Hamburg, Berlin, Bonn, 1997. Published in English as *U-boat Emblems of World War II 1939–1945*, Schiffer Military History, Atglen, 1999. An excellent work dealing with U-boat emblems, especially those which were painted on conning towers. Very well illustrated with drawings by the author who served as radio operator in *U30* and *U110*.

Hutson, Harry C.: *Grimsby's Fighting Fleet*; Hutton Press, Beverley, 1990.

Jones, Geoff: *The Month of the Lost U-boats*; William Kimber, London, 1977.

Jones, Geoff: *Autumn of the U-boats*; William Kimber, London 1984. About the autumn of 1943.

Jones, Geoff: *U-boat Aces*; William Kimber, London, 1984.

Jones, Geoff: *Defeat of the Wolf Packs*; William Kimber, London, 1986.

Jones, Geoff; *Submarines versus U-boats*; Wiliam Kimber, London, 1986.

Karschawin, Boris A.: *U250 – Neue Dokumente und Fakten*; St. Petersburg, 1994. Available from U-Boot-Archiv, 27478 Cuxhaven-Altenbruch. Please enclose at least two International Postal Reply Coupons if asking for details.

Kemp, Paul: *U-boats Destroyed*; Arms and Armor Press, London, 1997. Some of this book is superseded by more up-to-date information, but the explanations

for each boat are comprehensive and it is an easy to use as reference book.

Köhl, Fritz: *Vom Original zum Modell: Uboottyp XXI*; Bernard & Graefe Verlag, Koblenz, 1988.

Köhl, Fritz and Niestle, Axel; *Vom Original zum Modell: Uboottyp VIIC*; Bernard & Graefe Verlag, Koblenz, 1989.

Köhl, Fritz: *Vom Original zum Modell: Uboottyp IXC*; Bernard & Graefe Verlag, Koblenz, 1990.

Koop, Gerhard and Mulitze, Erich: *Die Marine in Wilhelmshaven*; Bernard & Graefe Verlag, Koblenz, 1987. Well illustrated and should also appeal to readers with only a small knowledge of German.

Koop, Gerhard and Galle, K and Klein F.; *Von der Kaiserlichen Werft zum Marinearsenal*; Bernard & Graefe Verlag, Munich, 1982. A fascinating and very well illustrated history of the naval base in Wilhelmshaven.

Lohmann, W. and Hildebrand, H.H.: *Die deutsche Kriegsmarine 1939 – 1945*; Podzun, Dorheim, 1956 – 1964. This multi-volume work is the standard reference document on the German Navy, giving details of ships, organisation and personnel.

Mattes, Klaus: *Die Seehunde*; E. S. Mittler & Sohn, Hamburg, Berlin, Bonn, 1995. A detailed account about midget U-boats, especially Type Seehund. Well illustrated.

Meister, Jürg: *Der Seekrieg in den osteuropäischen Gewässern 1941-1945*; J. F. Lehmanns, Munich, 1958.

Merten, Karl-Friedrich and Baberg, Kurt : *Wir Ubootfahrer sagen 'Nein – So war das nicht'*; J. Reiss Verlg, Grossaitingen, 1986.

Metzler, Jost: *The Laughing Cow*; William Kimber, London, 1955.

Möller, Eberhard; *Kurs Atlantik*; Motorbuch Verlag, Stuttgart, 1995.

Moore, Captain Arthur R.: *A careless word... a needless sinking*; American Merchant Marine Museum, Maine, 1983. A detailed and well illustrated account of ships lost during the war.

Mulligan, Timothy P.: *Neither Sharks Nor Wolves*; United States Naval Institute Press, Annapolis 1999 and Chatham

Publishing, London, 1999. An excellent book about the men who manned the U-boats.

Mulligan, Timothy P.: *Lone Wolf*; Praeger, Westport & London, 1993. An excellent account about the life and death of the U-boat ace Werner Henke of *U515*.

Niestle, Axel: *German U-boat Losses during World War II*; Greenhill, London, 1998. Well researched with up-to-date basic information, but lacking explanations and badly laid out, making it difficult to use as reference book.

OKM (Supreme Naval Command): *Bekleidungs und Anzugsbestimmungen für die Kriegsmarine*; Berlin, 1935; reprinted Jak P. Mallmann Showell, 1979. The official dress regulations of the German Navy.

OKM *Rangliste der deutschen Kriegsmarine*; Mittler & Sohn, published annually, Berlin.

OKM *Handbuch für U-boot-Kommandanten*; Berlin, 1942. Translated during the war and published by Thomas Publications, Gettysburg, 1989 as *The U-boat Commander's Handbook*.

Peillard, Leonce: *U-boats to the Rescue*; Jonathan Cape Ltd., London, 1963.

Plottke, Herbert: *Fächer Loos! (U172 in Einsatz)*; Podzun-Pallas, Wölfersheim-Berstadt, 1997.

Preston, Anthony: *U-boats*; Bison Books, London, 1978. Well illustrated with good photographs.

Prien, Günther: *U-boat Commander*; Tempus Publishing, Stroud, 2000. A reprint of this well known book by the commander of *U47*, although some of the comments must be taken with great pinch of salt and were probably not written by Prien.

Raeder, Dr. Erich: *Struggle for the Sea*; William Kimber, London 1966.

Raeder, Dr. Erich: *My Life*; US Naval Institute Press, 1960.

Reintjes, Karl Heinrich: *U524 – Das Kriegstagebuch eines U-bootes*; Ernst Knoth, Melle, 1994. A well annotated copy of the boat's log book.

Robertson, Terrence: *The Golden*

Horseshoe: Tempus Publishing, Stroud, 2000. A reprint of this early classic about *U99* and Otto Kretschmer.

Rohde, Jens: *Die Spur des Löwen – U1202*: Libri Books on Demand, Itzehoe, 2000. Most of this interesting book contains pictures and facsimiles, meaning it is not too difficult for people with only a smattering of German.

Rohwer, J.: *Axis Submarine Successes of World War II 1939-45*: Greenhill, London, 1998.

Rohwer, J.: *Uboote: Eine Chronik in Bildern*: Gerhard Stalling Verlag, Oldenburg, 1962.

Rohwer, J.: *U107*: Profile Publications, Windsor, 1971.

Rohwer, J.: *The Critical Convoy Battles of March 1943*: Ian Allan, London, 1977.

Rohwer, J. and Hümmelchen, G.: *Chronology of the War at Sea 1939-1945*: Greenhill, London, 1992. A good, solid and informative work. Well indexed and most useful for anyone studying the war at sea.

Rössler, Eberhard: *Die deutschen Uboote und ihre Werften*: Bernard & Graefe, Koblenz, 1979.

Rössler, Eberhard: *Geschichte des deutschen Ubootbaus*: Bernard & Graefe, Koblenz, 1986.

Rössler, Eberhard: *The U-boat*: Arms and Armor Press, London, 1981.

Schaeffer, Heinz: *U-boat 977*: William Kimber, London, 1952.

Schenk, Robert: *What it was like to be a sailor in World War II*: Naval Institute Press, Annapolis.

Schlemm, Jürgen: *Der U-Boot-Krieg 1939-1945 in der Literatur*: Elbe-Spree-Verlag, Hamburg and Berlin, 2000. A comprehensive bibliography of publications about the U-boat war.

Schmoeckel, Helmut: *Menschlichkeit im Seekrieg?*: E. S. Mittler Verlag, Herford, 1987.

Schulz, Wilhelm: *Über dem nassen Abgrund*: E. S. Mittler & Sohn, Berlin, Bonn and Herford, 1994. The story of *U124* by one of her commanders.

Sharpe, Peter: *U-boat Fact File*: Midland Publishing, Leicester, 1998. A handy reference book, well laid out and easy to use.

Showell, Jak P. Mallmann: *The German Navy in World War Two*: Arms and Armor Press, London, 1979; Naval Institute Press, Annapolis 1979 and translated as *Das Buch der deutschen Kriegsmarine*, Motorbuch Verlag, Stuttgart, 1982. Covers history, organisation, the ships, code writers, naval charts and a section on ranks, uniforms, awards and insignias by Gordon Williamson. Named by the United States Naval Institute as 'One of the Outstanding Naval Books of the Year'.

Showell, Jak P. Mallmann: *U-boats under the Swastika*: Ian Allan, Shepperton, 1973; Arco, New York, 1973 and translated as *Uboote gegen England*, Motorbuch, Stuttgart, 1974. A well illustrated introduction to the German U-boat Arm, which is now one of the longest selling naval books in Germany.

Showell, Jak P. Mallmann: *U-boats under the Swastika*: Ian Allan, London, 1987. A second edition with different photos and new text of the above title.

Showell, Jak P. Mallmann: *U-boat Command and the Battle of the Atlantic*: Conway Maritime Press, London, 1989; Vanwell, New York, 1989. A detailed history based on the U-boat Command's war diary.

Showell, Jak P. Mallmann: *Germania International*: Journal of the German Navy Study Group. Now out of print.

Showell, Jak P. Mallmann: *U-boat Commanders and Crews*: The Crowood Press, Marlborough, 1998.

Showell, Jak P. Mallmann: *German Navy Handbook 1939–1945*: Sutton Publishing, Stroud, 1999.

Showell, Jak P. Mallmann: *U-boats in Camera 1939–1945*: Sutton Publishing, Stroud, 1999.

Showell, Jak P. Mallmann: *Enigma U-boats*, Ian Allan; London 2000.

Showell, Jak P. Mallmann: *U-boats at War —Landings on Hostile Shores*: Ian Allan, London, 2000.

Showell, Jak P. Mallmann: *Atlantic U-boat Bases*: Sutton Publishing, Stroud, 2001.

Stärk, Hans: *Marineunteroffizierschule*: Plön—Holstein.

Stern, Robert C.: *Type VII U-boats*: Brockhampton Press, London, 1991.

Topp, Erich: *Fackeln über dem Atlantik*: Ullstein, Berlin, 1999. An autobiography by a famous U-boat commander.

U-Boot-Archiv: *Das Archiv* (German), *The U-boat Archive* (English language); a journal published twice a year for members of FTU, U-Boot-Archiv, Bahnhofstrasse 57, D-27478 Cuxhaven-Altenbruch. Please enclose at least two International Postal Reply Coupons if asking for details.

Verband Deutscher Ubootsfahrer: *Schaltung Küste*: Journal of the German Submariners' Association.

Wagner, Gerhard (editor): *Lagevorträge des Oberbefehlshabers der Kriegsmarine vor Hitler*: J. F. Lehmanns, Munich, 1972. Translated as *Fuehrer Conferences on Naval Affairs*. Greenhill, London, reprinted with new introduction 1990. The first English language edition was published before the German version.

Westwood, David: *Type VIIC*: Conway Maritime Press, London, 1974.

White, John F.: *U-boat Tankers 1941-45*: Airlife Publishing, Shrewsbury, 1998.

Williamson, Gordon: *The Iron Cross*: Blandford Press, Poole, 1986.

Williamson, Gordon: *The Knight's Cross of the Iron Cross*: Blandford, Poole, 1987.

Williamson, Gordon and Pavlovik, Darko: *U-boat Crews 1914-45*: Osprey, London, 1995. An interesting book with excellent colour drawings and black/white photographs.

Witthöft, Hans Jürgen: *Lexikon zur deutschen Marinegeschichte*: Koehler, Herford, 1977. An excellent two volume encyclopaedia.

Wynn, Kenneth: *U-boat Operations of the Second World War*: Chatham, London, 1997.

Zienert, J.: *Unsere Marineuniform*: Helmut Gerhard Schulz, Hamburg, 1970. The standard work about German naval uniforms.